CYCLE A
CELEBRATIONS
OF THE
WORD
FOR CHILDREN

CYCLE A
CELEBRATIONS
OF THE
WORD
FOR CHILDREN

WRITTEN BY BERNICE STADLER

EDITED BY NANCY REECE

TWENTY-THIRD PUBLICATIONS

Mystic, Connecticut

Third Printing 1989

Twenty-Third Publications
P.O. Box 180
185 Willow Street
Mystic, CT 06355
(203) 536-2611

Library of Congress Catalog Card Number 86-50864
ISBN 0-89622-308-6

To Father John Acri for sharing his love of Scripture with us and encouraging us to share our talents with others. Because of his openness to the Spirit, these children's celebrations were first developed.

To our pastor, Father Patrick Devine, for his constant support. Because of his vision and confidence, these scripts are being shared with others.

To the dedicated members of the Children's Liturgy Committee at St. John Neumann Church. Their love and hard work have produced some memorable moments in our parish. They have truly helped spread the good news of the gospel to our children.

CONTENTS

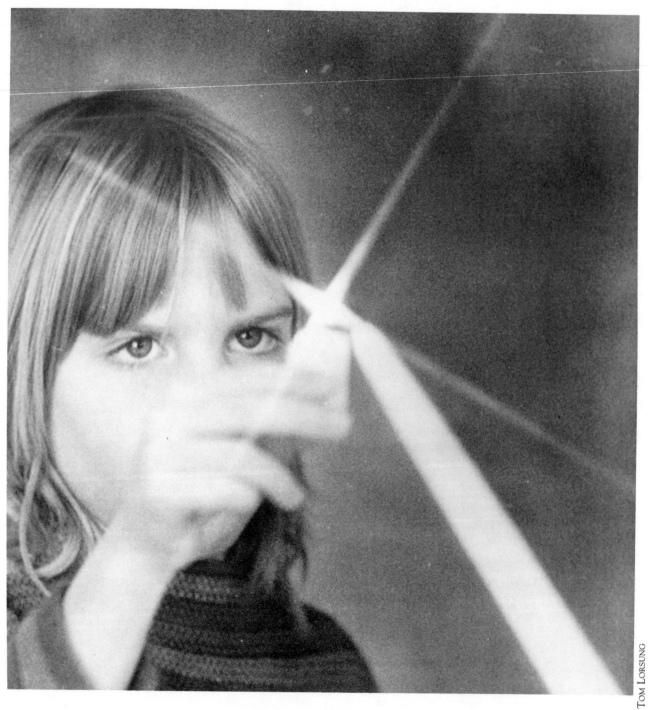

INTRODUCTION

The word of God that we hear each Sunday should be truly good news—to guide us, strengthen us, comfort us. But do our children agree? During the Eucharist, or even during instruction at home or in the classroom, do children experience the good news of Scripture and the lesson? We feared not. We feared that, for the most part in a typical adult-oriented service, the children have "tuned out." Perhaps the ideas presented are too sophisticated, wordy, or don't apply to the child's life. Or the presentation is so standard a child is tempted to daydream through it.

Our concern that children were not really part of our worship rituals culminated six years ago in the formation of the Children's Liturgy Committee in our church. With families with younger children in mind, the committee began planning once-a-month Masses directed at and including such families in the services. Because members of the committee wanted our children to appreciate and understand God's word, the Masses were designed to use children in many roles: as Scripture readers, as song leaders, as actors in dramatic presentations of the gospels, and as participants in the homily discussion.

Since its formation, the committee has met dozens of times sharing ideas, brainstorming, and creating services that focus on children's understanding of the teachings of the church. The response to these celebrations has been excellent. Every two to three years we survey the congregation attending the children's liturgies (approximately 500 adults and children) to see if this style of liturgy is still appreciated and desired. So far so good!

Although created in a liturgical setting, the 18 celebrations contained in this book are not designed to be used in one setting exclusively. They may be used in a classroom situation, or when instruction takes place in a private home, or they can be adapted for use in a liturgical setting. Our hope is that, however used, these celebrations will make religious ritual more accessible to children.

Glancing through the services, the reader will notice that the lessons are prepared in detail for an adult Presenter, with cues for the Presenter's motions and responses of the children. In our experience, Presenters appreciate knowing what is expected of them, what is the message or attitude to be developed with the children, and "What am I to do with this prop?" If presiding adults are not comfortable with what is planned, they can make changes that are compatible with their personalities.

To liven up the celebration, remembering it is for children, we use a variety of lessons methods. One of our favorites is storytelling. Doesn't everyone love a story? Using an opaque projector (our public schools allow us to use theirs) we enlarge the pictures in the children's literature book we are using, cut them out of poster board, and color them with bright paints or markers.

Tape roles are adhered to the back sides. The pictures are placed on the floor around our large easel (a parishioner made one to hold a 4' ×6' flannel-covered board). Two prepared students put up and take down the appropriate pictures while the Presenter narrates the story. We also use transparencies of pictures with an overhead projector and screen while the story is narrated. The results, judging from the children's response, are worth our efforts.

Filmstrips (no longer than six minutes), puppets used by a Presenter who is a bit of an actor, props, actors "walking on" to help with the lesson—all of these create an activity children respond to. Other patterns in the celebrations—the repeating aloud of Scripture names or learning sign language for a particular phrase—imprint the message of the lesson on the children's minds and hearts. After the lesson, hand-outs create a visual reminder of the gospel message. In our routine, supplies for making props and hand-outs are given to the committee members a month before the celebration.

In our community, after the scripts are typed, the committee chairperson and the member in charge for that specific service meet with the Presenter. They talk through the service, demonstrating sign language or motions with props. Last minute changes are made and reported back to the committee. Every committee member has a copy of the script and is expected to know who is in charge of details like lights, cueing actors, music, filmstrips, passing hand-outs, etc. In the case of liturgical use, scripts are also given to the organist and adult cantors two weeks before the service.

The list of Scriptural readings in each section identifies this particular Sunday in Cycle A. Since these celebrations are not strictly intended for use at Sunday Eucharist, all three readings are not included in the service. In some of the services, the gospel reading is rewritten as a dramatization or narration. In others, the Presenter simply reads the gospel from a Bible. To shorten the service because it is for children, we prefer including just the First Reading and the Gospel. In our experience, we have learned to choose older children (sixth grade and older) as Readers, Prayer Leaders, and speaking actors, and children in fifth grade and above in the non-speaking roles. We realize that many younger children would love to speak parts or lead a prayer, and their mothers would love it, but for the most part working with the older children produces smoother practices and more meaningful services. The younger children, then, look forward to their own participation.

In our parish, at the beginning of each celebration, children pass out song sheets with words to all the songs we will be singing, and programs with responses to the prayers. We try to keep the commotion down, setting a mood of reverence by playing recorded music we will use again during the service. We do not practice songs before the service—feeling that's like having a dry run of "Happy Birthday" in front of the birthday child! But in this and other ways, the celebrations are flexible, adaptable to particular situations and preferences. To encourage all the children to participate, we suggest two songs in each service, indicating sources in parentheses after the song title. Our suggestions, of course, can be replaced with other favorites. For our part, we have included music we know children like, not always liturgical in nature but cheerful, upbeat songs that are easy to learn.

The abbreviations identifying sources for particular songs refer to *Hi God I and II, Bloom Where You Are Planted* (BWYAP), and *Color the World With Song.* (CTWWS). All three are albums by Carey Landry available from North American Liturgical Resources (NALR), 10802 N. 23rd

Avenue Pheonix, AZ 85029. "Little People's Scripture Stories" episode 10 is available from Roa Films and Video, 914 N. Fourth Street, P.O. Box 661, Milwaukee, WI 53201. Permission to quote from *Everything You Need for Children's Worship* by Jack Noble White (© 1978) is granted by St. Anthony Messenger Press, 1615 Republic Street, Cincinnati, OH 45210. All rights reserved. "Growing to Glow" by Sr. Mary Chupein, S.F.C.C. was originally published in *Service* by the Missionary Society of St. Paul the Apostle in the State of New York. Used by permission of Paulist Press.

In our parish these children-oriented services, whether presented in church, in a classroom or in a home answer in part our concern that children are "tuning out" during adult-directed services. We hope these 18 celebrations will answer similar needs in other parishes and will inspire more creative efforts on behalf of and by children.

BERNICE STADLER
·NANCY REECE

St. John Neumann Church
Lancaster, Penn.

New Kingdom Coming

(Second Sunday of Advent—Winter)

Isaiah 11: 1-10, Romans 15: 4-9, Matthew 3: 1-12

THEME
: The reign of God is justice and peace. It has come. Reform your lives!

PROPS
: 1. Paper tree stump or a real one with a green tissue paper bud on a green pipe cleaner attached to it. Two free-standing paper trees, at least 5 feet in height (or large branches set in buckets and filled with plaster). These trees are set about 8 feet apart. Blue paper or fabric as "water" at least 2 feet deep is stretched between the trees. A metal tub filled with a bit of water is placed behind the "water," out of sight, with a small glass bowl inside. One of the trees should have some plastic or real apples attached to the branches.
: 2. The First Reading is done with four readers dressed as Old Testament characters. One of them is Isaiah. These readers may also be used as gospel actors.
: 3. Three poster-size pictures depicting scenes from the First Reading. These may be sketched or found in a Bible coloring book and enlarged. They are used in the lesson. They are 1) pictures of lamb lying with a wolf, 2) calf and a lion eating together, and 3) a baby boy sitting with a cobra. These may be made with cardboard supports on their backs to self-stand on the floor or they may be adhered to a wall.
: 4. Sign that says "Isaiah and John the Baptist"
: 5. Sign that says "Messenger of God"
: 6. Handouts—picture card of lamb and lion with words "His peace can be yours, prepare yourselves"

PERSONNEL
: 1. Presenter
: 2. Prayer leader
: 3. Song leader
: 4. Readers for the First Reading
: 5. Actors for the Gospel

GREETING

PRESENTER
: A new king is on the way! Let us prepare ourselves for his coming. The scripture today will help us get ready for Christmas—to prepare

our hearts for Jesus' birthday. Let us bow our heads for a moment and receive Jesus' presence.

OPENING PRAYER

PRAYER LEADER   Heavenly Father, through your prophets you promised us a Savior. One who would bring justice and peace-filled love. Thank you for sending Jesus. Through him we thank and praise you forever and ever. Amen.

FIRST READING
(adapted from Isaiah 11:1-10)

(This Reading will be proclaimed in choral in parts. The reader [dressed as Isaiah in a tunic or robe with a colorful sash tied diagonally across the chest] is alone near the stump. Two other readers [dressed in Old Testament fashion] are to Isaiah's left and right).

READER   All the kings of our people, Israel, were like branches stemming from the tree of Jesse, the father of the first true king, David. Our kingdom was conquered by enemies, however. You could say all that was left was a stump. But I, the prophet Isaiah, gave hope to my people in these sad times. A new king would come! You know him as Jesus.

ISAIAH: *(Walks to table and lifts lectionary and proclaims)* A reading from the Book of the Prophet Isaiah. On that day a shoot shall sprout from the stump of Jesse and from his roots a bud shall blossom. The spirit of the Lord shall rest upon him: a spirit of wisdom and of understanding, a spirit of counsel and of strength, a spirit of knowledge and of fear of the Lord, and his delight shall be the fear of the Lord.

READERS 2 & 3   Not by appearance shall he judge nor by hearsay shall he decide, but he shall judge the poor with justice, and decide a right for the lands afflicted. He shall strike the ruthless with the rod of his mouth, and with the breath of his lips he shall slay the wicked. Justice shall be the band around his waist, and faithfulness a belt upon his hips.

READER 4 & ISAIAH   *(Isaiah joins Reader 4)* Then the wolf shall be a guest of the lamb, and the leopard shall lie down with the kid;

READERS 2 & 3   The calf and the young lion shall browse together with a little child to guide them.

READER 4 & ISAIAH   The cow and the bear shall be neighbors together and their young shall rest; the lion shall eat hay like the ox.

READERS 2 & 3	The baby shall play by the cobra's den, and the child lay his hand on the adder's lair.
READER 4 & ISAIAH	There shall be no harm or ruin on all my holy mountain; for the earth shall be filled with knowledge of the Lord, as water covers the sea.
ISAIAH	On that day, the root of Jesse, set up as a signal for the nations, the Gentiles shall seek out, for his dwelling shall be glorious!
SONG LEADER	"Come, O Come, Emmanuel"

These simple verses lend themselves to sign language.

"Come"—both hands out, palms up.
"Lord"—right hand with thumb and index extended in L shape. Hand is drawn across chest diagonally beginning at left shoulder down to right waist.
"Jesus"—touch right middle finger to palm of the left hand and then repeat with the other hand.
"Born in our hearts"—cross arms over chest.
"Peace—hand in front of chest, fingertips touching in form of teepee, pull hands down and apart.

GOSPEL
(adapted from Matthew 3:1-12)

(The actors who are to be "baptized" sit near the trees and the water)

PRESENTER	Imagine that you are living in Judea, sitting near the River Jordan. You have heard about this preacher John the Baptist and you come to hear what he has to say.

A reading from the Holy Gospel according to Matthew

When John the Baptizer made his appearance as a preacher in the desert of Judea, this was his theme:

(Student dressed as John the Baptist walks in front of the water and addresses the people there and the whole group. He is dressed in a brown fur tunic with a belt. He has a leather pouch strapped across his chest. He is barefooted. His hands are raised and he uses as much emotion as possible without causing laughter.)

JOHN	"Reform your lives! The reign of God is at hand." *(When the presenter begins the next lines, John moves over to the small group sitting hear the water and waiting to be "baptized." He then walks behind the water design*

and begins "baptizing" one at a time. This is done by John standing on one side of the metal tub and the penitent on the other. Using a small glass dish, John pours water over the person's head while he or she kneels on one knee.)

PRESENTER: It was of him that the prophet Isaiah had spoken when he said, "A herald's voice in the desert: Prepare the way of the Lord. Make straight his path."

John was clothed in a garment of camel's hair and wore a leather belt around his waist. Grasshoppers and wild honey were his food. At that time Jerusalem, all Judea, and the whole region around the Jordon were going out to him. They were being baptized by him in the Jordan River, as they confessed their sins.

(Two actors dressed in fine clothes with high hats similar to a bishop's walk up to the water area. John sees them and stops.)

PRESENTER   When he saw that many of the Pharisees and Sadducees were stepping forward for his bath, he said *(John steps out from behind the water and points his finger at the Pharisees saying in an angry voice:)*

JOHN   You brood of vipers! Who told you to flee from the wrath to come? Give some evidence that you mean to reform. Do not pride yourselves on the claim, "Abraham is our father." I tell you, God can raise up children to Abraham from these very stones. Even now the ax is laid to the root of the tree. Every tree that is not fruitful *(he plucks a plastic or real apple from one of the trees and places it into his pouch)* will be cut down and thrown into the fire!" *(John sits down with his people while the Presentor finishes John's words)*

PRESENTER   John went on to say, "I baptize you in water for the sake of reform, but the one who will follow me is more powerful than I. I am not even fit to carry his sandals. He it is who will baptize you in the Holy Spirit and fire. His winnowing-fan in his hand, he will clear his threshing floor, and gather his grain into the barn, but the chaff he will burn in unquenchable fire."—This is the gospel of the Lord.

LESSON

PRESENTER   Today two prophets spoke to us. *(Hold up sign with their names Isaiah and John the Baptist)* Can you say their names? *(repeat)* Can anyone tell me what a prophet is? *(response)* They were *(hold up a sign saying Messengers of God)* messengers of God—not angels as at Christmas— but men and women who were called by God to give a message to his people.

Isaiah was a well-educated, refined prophet who lived about 600 years before Jesus. In the First Reading, Isaiah was giving hope to the people of Israel, promising them that a new bud will grow from the stump of Israel *(bend down to touch the bud)*. That's a fancy way of saying that a new king or Messiah will come. He will bring justice and peace. A peace that is unbelievable. Do you recall how he described it? Some of you have pictures of what he said. *(Take the large pictures from the students, one at a time, and mention what is depicted)* Lamb lying with a wolf, calf and a lion eating together, and baby boy sitting with a cobra.

Isaiah used these images of animals to describe the harmony. This peace-filled life that Isaiah speaks of is not just a better life, but a new wonderful life. How do you think that the people felt when Isaiah gave them this message. *(response)* Good! You bet!

Now, let's take a look at St. John the baptist. John, will you come up here? *(Presentor puts his arm around John.)* John was Jesus's cousin. This prophet had a different style of delivering his message. He seemed a bit strange, don't you agree. Who can remember—what did John wear? *(camel's hair)* and what did he eat? *(grasshoppers and honey!)* and where did he live? *(in the desert)* John, why did you live so differently?

JOHN I couldn't live in the city. I felt closer to God in the desert. Only one thing was important to me. To prepare the people for the Promised One.

PRESENTER John felt called by God to "shake the people up." He believed that the new king, the Messiah that Isaiah promised, was here now.

JOHN Most of the people thought that the age of justice and peace would come no matter what kind of lives they lived. As long as they were Jewish, sons of Abraham, they thought they had it made. But I told them that's not so! I told them to shape up! Reform their lives.

PRESENTER John, you were very angry at those Pharisees and Sadducees in our Gospel. Why?

JOHN They were religious phonies...they acted holy and followed the laws that people could see, but inside they didn't really love God and his people. They didn't want to reform.

PRESENTER Children, how do you think John wanted the people to change their lives? *(response suggestions—being kind, giving up bad habits, no lying)*

Thank you John. *(John sits down.)* It's good to hear the message of both prophets during this time of Advent. We, like Isaiah's people, are happy that Jesus, the shoot of Jesse, came into our world to bring justice and peace and that he will come again. And like John's people we need to be "shaken up" a bit, warned to reform our lives especially during this preparation of Christmas.

We have a reminder of today's lesson. It's a picture card of the Lamb and the Lion with the words "His peace can be yours, prepare yourselves." You will receive one as you return to your seats.

COMMUNAL PRAYER

PRAYER LEADER

To our requests, please respond, "Hear us, O Lord."

Lord, may our homes be places of support and forgiveness rather than argument and criticism so that our homes will be ready to welcome you, we pray to the Lord...Hear us, O Lord.

Lord, help me to take a good look at myself. Let me see how I don't act as Jesus wishes so as John said, *"I too may reform," we pray to the Lord...Hear us, O Lord.*

Lord, we pray for our world. We are its caretakers. Help us to bring peace, to share its gifts with all peoples, we pray to the Lord...Hear us, O Lord.

SONG LEADER

"Come, Lord Jesus" (Hi God II)

Jesus, Light of the World

(Christmas—Winter)

Isaiah 52: 7-10, Hebrews 1: 1-6, John 1:1-18

THEME
Jesus the light of the world is born!

PROPS
1. Children have been asked the week before to bring gifts of socks, mittens, and nutritious snacks and place them in a basket in the sanctuary.
2. Large basket to hold gifts
3. A "house front" made of heavy cardboard is placed up front. It should have a sheer curtain doorway.
4. A cardtable bush (green paper attached to four sides of cardtable) Underneath is a "log fire" (logs nailed together, spotlight covered with cellophane).
5. A lectern to the left of the bush. Reader will light one candle and do the beginning reading from there.
6. A large cardboard donkey on wheels
7. Three spotlights, one in back of house, one in front of house, and one near the campfire. (This celebration begins in darkness with a guitarist sitting on a stool in spotlight singing a solo. Lights are turned on when titles of God are echoed by the actors.)
8. Small birthday cake with large number candles 1 9 8 6
9. Handout for children—a small candle with the first reading attached
10. The children that echo during the first reading should stand in groups of three in the back corners.
11. Doll and doll bed used for baby Jesus
12. Wooden crates for Mary and Joseph in front of the house front. Knitting for Mary and carving items for Joseph
13. Gift-wrapped bag labeled "Thankfulness" and a box labeled "Hope" to be used during Lesson
14. A large red paper heart necklace used during Lesson

PERSONNEL
1. Presenter
2. Prayer leader
3. Adult Guitarist/Song leader
4. Reader

5. Actors to play the following parts: Mary, Joseph, Isaac, Rachel, Innkeeper, Wife, Four Shepherds, Six Angels
6. Six children to do the echo during the First Reading (shepherds may be used here)
7. Child to present Birthday Cake during Lesson
8. Three children to present gifts of thankfulness, hope, and a large red heart (generosity)

OPENING PRAYER

This celebration begins in darkness, with song leader sitting on stool singing "Violet in the Snow," verses 1 and 2 (Hi God II).

READER   *(Lights one candle and recites the First Reading)* The people who walked in darkness have seen a great light; on those who live in a land of deep shadow a light has shone. *(Lights on Note: This is the reading attached to candle used as handout)*

READER   *(With much expression and power)* For there is a child born for us, a son given to us and dominion is laid on his shoulders; and this is the name they give him: Wonder Counselor *(First Echo repeat the words, as does Second Echo after a brief pause).*

READER   Mighty God *(First Echo and Second Echo each repeats in turn. The same is done with each name.)*

READER   Eternal Father

READER   Prince of Peace

PRAYER LEADER   What wondrous titles we have given our savior. Tonight we celebrate his birth. Let the celebration begin!

GREETING

PRESENTER   Merry Christmas, everyone! The waiting is over. Jesus is born again in our hearts. Before we go any further, let us join hands with our neighbors, close our eyes, and let the peace of Jesus fill us. *(Pause)* No matter what has happened today, let his peace fill us now. *(Pause again)*

SONG LEADER   Let us praise God with the first Christmas song that the angels began, "Angels We Have Heard on High."

GOSPEL
(adapted from John 1:1-18)

(The lights are turned out. Lectern is removed. Presenter stands next to the house where Joseph and Mary are sitting. A spotlight is used on each scene in turn.)

SCENE I

(The narrative begins with Mary and Joseph kissing one-year-old Jesus goodnight behind a sheer curtain doorway. Spotlight in back of house is on.)

MARY   Goodnight, Jesus. Sleep well. Now, don't get out of bed. Tomorrow is your special day. *(Mary and Joseph walk through the doorway. They sit on crates in front of house. Mary knits and Joseph sands and carve on a wood project. Back light is off. Front on.)*

MARY   Oh, Joseph. I can't believe Jesus is one year old already.

JOSEPH   The year has passed quickly here in Egypt. The Lord has been good to us, Mary. I hope we soon make the trip back home to Nazareth.

MARY   That was a long trip last year. Joseph, do you remember our neighbors, Isaac and Rachel, and how upset they were? *(Light is off)*

PRESENTER   In those days Caesar Augustus published a decree ordering a census to be taken of the whole Roman world. *(Light on Presenter is on)*

Everyone went to register, each to his own town. and so Joseph went from the town of Nazareth in Galilee to Judea into David's town of Bethlehem because he was of the same line as David. He went to register with Mary, his promised wife, who was with child. *(Light off)*

SCENE II

(Isaac, the traveler, is pulling a donkey up a ramp. His wife, Rachel, is walking behind. Light on.)

ISAAC   Come on, you ol' pile of bones! We still have many a mile to go on this wretched trip!

RACHEL   Isaac, Isaac, take it easy. Watch your blood pressure.

ISAAC   My blood pressure, you say? The Romans and their census don't care about my blood pressure. Why don't the Romans come to our towns and count us, instead of making us travel so far!!

RACHEL	Isaac, please stop complaining.
ISAAC	Why shouldn't I complain? Everyone here from Nazareth is complaining!
RACHEL	Not Mary and Joseph—and Mary is 9 month's pregnant!
ISAAC	Oh those two. They never complain about anything. They're different! *(Isaac begins to depart with the donkey down the ramp)*
RACHEL	They're different alright—different and happy—and kind—and helpful. *(Light off)*

SCENE III

JOSEPH	*(Light on Mary and Joseph)* It was my turn to be upset when we couldn't find a room for the night. I think we must have knocked on every door in Bethlehem.
MARY	Joseph, we must have looked a sorry sight for that innkeeper's wife to take pity on us and offer us her stable. *(Light off)*
PRESENTER	*(Light on Presenter)* While they were there the time came for Mary to have her child. She gave birth to her first-born son, wrapped him in swaddling clothes, and laid him in a manger, because there was no room for them at the inn.

SCENE IV

(The wife and innkeeper are dressed in nightshirts, holding candles. The wife is peering out an imaginary window. The innkeeper is standing a little behind her, rubbing his sleepy eyes.)

INNKEEPER	Why do you look out there, Ruth? What's so interesting?
WIFE	I'm looking at our stable where that Jewish couple are staying. Their light is still on. Why aren't they sleeping?
INNKEEPER	*(Patting wife on the back)* Come on, just admit it. You're feeling bad because you didn't offer them our home to stay in...she being pregnant and all.
WIFE	*(Angry, defending herself)* No, I'm not!! I gave them the use of our stable, didn't I? Am I supposed to offer my own bed? Let's be realistic!!
INNKEEPER	Well, I'm going back to bed, Ruth.

WIFE *(Peering out again)* I just wish I knew what was going on! *(Light off. Wife leaves the room taking the table with her, exposing campfire.)*

PRESENTER There were shepherds in the countryside, living in the fields and keeping night watch over their flocks. *(Four shepherds position themselves around fire)*

There was the angel of the Lord appeared to them as the glory of the Lord shone around them. The shepherds were very much afraid.

The angel said to them: "You have nothing to fear! I come to proclaim good news to you—tidings of great joy to be shared by the whole people. This day in David's city, a savior has been born to you, the Messiah and Lord! Let this be a sign to you: You will find the infant wrapped in swaddling clothes and..."

SCENE V

(Four shepherds are gathered around a fire. The spotlight, covered with red cellophone and nestled in the logs of wood, is on.)

SHEPHERD 1 "...and lying in a manger...wrapped in swaddling clothes and lying in a manger."—that's what he said.

SHEPHERD 2 Sure, sure—in a manger. Some dream you had! The Messiah's birth announced to shepherds, the low-life of Bethlehem.

SHEPHERD 3 It's true. It was over there on the third hill.

SHEPHERD 4 Wake up!! There is no messiah. No savior for us. Just work and being pushed around by the Romans.

SHEPHERD 1 The prophets promised a savior to come. I believe it. I believe the messenger.

PRESENTER Suddenly there was with the angel a multitude of the heavenly host. *(Six angels with their arms raised encircle shepherds)*

SONG LEADER Gloria in Excelsis Deo (refrain from "*Angels We Have Heard on High*")

PRESENTER The shepherd went quickly into Bethlehem and found the baby lying in a manger. *(Head angel takes hand of shepherd as they exit.)* Once they saw they understood what the angels told them. They returned glorifying and praising God for all they had seen and heard.—This is the gospel of the Lord.

LESSON

PRESENTER (*Lectern is moved near the Presenter*) How many of us are feeling happy tonight? Raise your hands. Are you excited? (*response*) Looks like most of our hearts are in good shape.

We can't say that for some of the characters in our gospel story. Some of them had "heart trouble"—trouble with their attitudes. I think they can teach us something.

Take Isaac the Traveler. (*Isaac rises from the group and stands next to the presenter*) What was the matter, Isaac?

ISAAC I was a complainer—I grumbled all the time.

PRESENTER (*Puts arm around Isaac*) Poor Isaac, something was missing in his heart. He wasn't thankful, was he? On this Christmas Eve and for as long as we can, we won't complain. We will thank God and praise each other. Isaac, we have a gift for you—for your heart. It's a bag full of thankfulness. (*Gets gift from a child in the group and presents it to Isaac*)

ISAAC (*Gives thanks and sits down*)

PRESENTER Where's Ruth, the innkeeper's wife? (*She stands with the presenter*) Why were you so agitated?

RUTH My conscience was bothering me, I guess. Mary and Joseph needed my help and I wasn't generous.

PRESENTER She wasn't generous. I guess Ruth's heart was just a little too small. We can be selfish like that sometimes but not tonight. Tonight we share our gifts (*motions to the gifts in the basket*). We bring presents of snacks, socks and mittens for our needy brothers and sisters in the city. Ruth, our generosity will help your heart grow. (*Gets large heart necklace from child in group and places it over Ruth's head*) Perhaps it will grow this big, Ruth.

RUTH (*Gives thanks and sits down*)

PRESENTER Rufus the Shepherd, where are you? (*Shepherd stands next to Presenter.*) What was wrong with your heart?

RUFUS I don't know how it happened, but I lost hope. I didn't believe in God's promise that a Savior would come."

PRESENTER Rufus didn't believe anymore. (*Extends arms to the children*) I ask all of you, do you believe in Jesus! (*Yes*) Do you have hope in your hearts?

	(Yes) Let's give Rufus a big box of Hope this Christmas. *(Gets box of Hope from child in group)*
RUFUS	*(Gives thanks and sits down)*
PRESENTER	Our hearts are to be like these candles (indicating lit candles in the sanctuary) spreading light and goodwill into the darkness. Raise your hands if you believe that you can do that—spread light and goodwill into the darkness. Yes, you can, because Jesus, the light of the world, is born in your hearts.

We have a gift for you. Each of you will receive a small candle *(shows the gift)* with the prayer you heard first at this celebration. Before you go to sleep tonight, get the family to sit down, light your candles, and pray this prayer together, welcoming the light of the world into your homes.

Before you return to your seats we have some special candles to light, those on Jesus' birthday cake. *(A child presents the birthday cake)* We've been celebrating Jesus' birthday for 1986 years *(indicating the numbered candles 1 9 8 6—lights the candles)* Let us all sing Happy Birthday to Jesus. *(Asks a child to blow out the candles after singing.)* We're going to give this cake as a gift to a needy family along with our other gifts. Okay, children, my helpers will give you your little candles as you return to your seats. I ask you to only take one per family. *(Props are removed as the children return to their seats)*

COMMUNAL PRAYER

PRAYER LEADER	To our petitions please respond, "Jesus, be our light."

Jesus, give us the strength to spread your good will in the world, we pray to the Lord…Jesus, be our light.

May we see you, Jesus, in our Moms, Dads, brothers and sisters—in our friends and enemies, we pray to the Lord…Jesus, be our light.

For those people in the world who are hungry, sad, and lonely on this night, we pray to the Lord…Jesus, be our light.

For our parish, that we may truly care for and support each other, we pray to the Lord…Jesus, be our light.

SONG LEADER	"Hark, the Herald Angels Sing"

Christ Is Born to All

(Christmas—Winter)

Isaiah 52: 7-10, Hebrews 1: 1-6, Luke 2: 1-14

THEME   Christ is born to everyone in the world.

PROPS

1. Chasuble and stole decorated by the children (if used in Liturgy)
2. Eight flags of different nations
3. Paper mache rocks
4. Large red heart pillow
5. Doll and blanket
6. Birthday cupcakes with small party flags inserted for all the children
7. Hooded "traveling cloak" and lantern for Presenter.
8. One candle and matches for each family
9. All children will be bringing gifts for baby Jesus—socks, nutritious snack or a toy. They should be told the week before Christmas.

PERSONNEL

1. Presenter
2. Prayer leader
3. Song leader
4. Mary, shown pregnant with tied pillow
5. Joseph
6. Six children to remove rocks
7. Eight children to carry flags
8. One child to carry heart pillow
9. Three angels

GREETING

PRAYER LEADER   Tonight is a Holy Night, a Silent Night. Let us quiet ourselves and wait for Jesus to be among us *(waits until relatively quiet)*.

PRESENTER   *(wearing a hooded cloak, carrying a lantern, Presenter walks in front of group)* Many roads are traveled, some are rocky, and some are smooth, others are dusty and dry. Many times we give no thought at all to which road we are traveling, but today we all ask the same question "Is this the road to Bethlehem?" *(moving lantern about as if to see better)*. Our journey is dark; Jesus will light it.

SONG LEADER	Families please light your candles so that we may see our way, and let us sing "It's a Small World" (from *The Official Album of Disneyland and Walt Disney World. After the song, the lights are turned on and the candles extinguished.*)
	Thank you. Our path is lit. Please blow out your candles.

OPENING PRAYER

PRESENTER	We have found rocks on our path to Bethlehem! Who put them here?
CHILD 1	As we make the journey to Bethlehem, we confess we have not always done our best. We have put rocks and bumps in the road with our selfishness.
CHILD 2	We have not listened to God's Word. We have not been as helpful to our parents and our teachers and our friends as we could be.
CHILD 1	We have not thought much about sick and lonely people and tried to comfort them. We have wanted our own way a lot of the time.
CHILD 2	We are sorry for our selfishness and want to do better. We will remove the rocks from our way.
PRESENTER	*(Pauses, while children remove rocks)* Our Path is cleared. But where is Bethlehem? Where is the stable? Do we find it in pretty statues? In Christmas cards? It's been 1986 years since Jesus was born!! *(acting decisively).* We must make a new Bethlehem here, now.
CHILD 1	What city shall he be born in?
PRESENTER	All the cities of every country.
SONG LEADER	Repeat "It's a Small World" *(Eight children bring up eight flags of different nations, place them in the stands provided and announce the country they represent. They will remain standing behind the flags until the end of the song . . . then they return to their seats. Flags can be made of fabric colored with fabric paint or crayons—or they may be made of poster board.)*

GOSPEL

PRESENTER	Luke 2:1-14 *(As the gospel is read, Mary and Joseph walk up and kneel in the center of the flags, placing the baby on the pillow. Joseph takes a blanket off of his arm and tucks the baby in. Three angels kneel around them.)*—This is the gospel of the Lord.

LESSON

PRESENTER   Thank you, children, for helping with the gospel (*motioning to Angels, Mary, and Joseph*). How about sitting here by me for now.

If we would come to the manger at Bethlehem, we would bring gifts. We might bring clothes to keep the baby warm. Some of you children here brought socks as your Christmas gift. Please bring them up now and place them around the baby, and then sit here. Some of you have brought a yummy treat to share with Jesus. Please bring these up (*repeats procedure*) and some of you have brought a toy—please come up. All of us have bright smiles and warm hearts to share with the baby, so will the rest of the children please come up.

Let's wish Jesus and everyone here a Merry Christmas—but not in English. Let's try to say it in the language of our Spanish brothers and sisters; Feliz Navidad (*Fey-leese nav-ee-dod*). Can you sat that? (*Repeat this procedure for these languages:*)

> French—Joyeux Noelle (Jwa yu No el)
> German—Fröhliche Weinachten (Fro-leek-ta Vine nok ten)
> Russian—(Cristos vas Do acja)
> Japanese—(Karisumasu)

Good, you did that very well. Now in our English, Let's have just the children sing "Happy Birthday" to Jesus.

You know we really don't give all these gifts to the baby Jesus, but we can give them to his needy children.

Wouldn't it be great to sit by the manger, to touch the baby Jesus? You can touch him you know! Raise your hand and go like this (*raises hand and touches cheek*). There, you have touched the Lord. Now put your arm out and place it on the person next to you. You have again touched the child Jesus. Jesus is right here now in you and me.

Now go and give the Baby Jesus a kiss tonight by kissing your Mom and Dad, or someone special that you may have brought with you today when you return to your seats.

COMMUNAL PRAYER

PRAYER LEADER   At this Christmas celebration we come before God to ask him for all our needs.

Today we will ask God together. The right side of the room will read aloud their first petition. The center will read the second and the left the third. Our response will be "Emmanuel, hear us."

FIRST   Lord, our world needs peace. You have given it to us, but we have hidden it. Help us find that peace. We pray to the Lord...Emmanuel, hear us.

SECOND   Lord, our world needs justice. We are all your children, none greater than the other. Help us to be just. We pray to the Lord...Emmanuel, hear us.

THIRD   Lord, our world needs joy, the true joy that only you and your word can bring. Help us to discover it in our lives. We pray to the Lord...Emmanuel, hear us.

SONG LEADER   "Come, Lord Jesus" (Hi God II)

ing for Christ

er)
ans 3: 2-3, 5-6, Matthew 2: 1-12

agi? Like them, are we aware of signs of Jesus'
for truth?

have been told the week before to bring a used
ge with another child.)

with the blessing of the home written on each—
his house that in it there may be health, hap-
, humility, forgiveness, mercy and peace. May
in upon this house and upon all who gather
chalk is taped to each star.
rrh symbols

7. Flannelboard figures of Herod, Three Wise Men, Priest with scroll,
Three Scribes, Three Wise Men on Camels, should be 15″ to 18″
tall. Glue flannel strips at intervals on the back of the pictures.

SIGNS
1. "Epiphany"
2. "19 C-M-B87"

PERSONNEL
1. Presenter
2. Prayer leader
3. Song leader
4. Reader
5. Trumpeter
6. Three Kings
7. Two children to work at flannelboard

GREETING

TRUMPETER   *(Standing in the middle of the room plays "Entrance Call" and says:)* Hear
ye, Hear ye. Now entering with (Name of Presenter), the Three Wise
Men, astrologers from the East in search of the Messiah! All children
who have brought a book to exchange, please walk behind the kings

in our procession, leaving your books in the basket. *(Process around room while singing "We Three Kings")*

PRESENTER   Welcome on this Feast of the Epiphany. In the Scriptures today we find ourselves in the shoes of the Wise Men looking for signs of God, searching for truth. Some of the children brought a book to exchange, a sign of their search for knowledge. So, as we begin this celebration, let us pray to God.

OPENING PRAYER

PRAYER LEADER   God, our caring Father, we thank you today not only for giving us your son, Jesus, but also for giving signs in our lives that point the way to him, lest we go astray. It is through Jesus in union with the Holy Spirit that we will always praise you forever and ever. Amen.

FIRST READING

READER   Isaish 60: 1-6

SONG LEADER   "Whenever Two or More" *(Sunrise in the Dead of Winter, Ray Repp)*

GOSPEL NARRATIVE
(adapted from Matthew 2: 1-12)

PRESENTER   Gather around. The feast we're celebrating today is called the Epiphany. *(Places sign on flannelboard)* Can you say that? *(Says it with them)* It's sometimes called the Twelfth Night because it's twelve days after Christmas.

Our Gospel story is about three men—sometimes called Wise Men, magi, astrologers or even kings. Although we're not sure, it has been said their names were Caspar, Melchoir, and Balthasar *(repeats names with children)*. They were searching for someone. You can help me tell this story with this big flannelboard.

(Herod and three Wise Men on the board.) During the days when Jesus was born in Bethlehem of Judea, Herod was king. Astrologers from the east came to Jerusalem. They met with King Herod and they asked him, "Where is the newborn king of the Jews? We have seen his star, and we have come to worship him." King Herod couldn't answer, and said he would talk with them later. *(Three Wise Men are removed and three scribes and priest are put up)*

Hearing this news from the Wise Men disturbed King Herod and the people of Jerusalem. Gathering the chief priests and scribes King Herod asked them where the Messiah was to be born.

The chief priest said, "He's to be born in Bethlehem of Judea." The prophets wrote, The Prophets wrote, "You, "Bethlehem, land of Judah, are small but important, for from you shall come a leader who will care for my people Israel. The Messiah will be born there."

King Herod met the astrologers again, this time in secret... *(removes all the figures and puts up King Herod and three Wise Men)*. He learned when the star had appeared. Then he sent them on their way. "Go to Bethlehem and search for the child. When you have found Him, bring me word that I too may go and worship Him."

The astrologers continued on their way... *(removes all the figures and puts up three Wise Men on camels, town, star and tree)*. The star which they had seen in the east went before them till it came to rest over the place where the child was. "What joy fills my heart as I see this star!" said one of the Wise Men. "Let us enter this house to see the child!"

They entered the house *(removes all the figures and puts up the Three Wise Men giving gifts, Mary and Jesus)*. The astrologers fell to their knees and worshipped the child. "We bring treasures—gifts of great value."

Being warned in a dream not to return to King Herod, the astrologers returned to their own country by another route—This is the gospel of the Lord.

LESSON

PRESENTER   So who were the Wise Men searching for? *(Jesus)* Do you think King Herod really wanted to go and worship Jesus too? No, I don't think so. He was the king and he didn't want any "new-born king of the Jews" butting in on his power. How did the Wise Men find Jesus? *(followed the star)* Yes, they knew the meaning of the star. They were looking for a sign. The star would lead them to the Messiah.

Do you think you would be good at interpreting signs? Let's see...

If you were looking to see if a rabbit had been in your yard one snowy day, what sign would you look for? *(response)*

If you were outside playing on this snowy day and you smelled wood burning, how could you determine which house is using its fireplace? *(response)*

If you woke up in the morning and wanted to know if it rained last night, what would you look for? *(response)*

Here's a tough one: We believe that Jesus lives in our families, in our homes. What are some signs you would look for that indicate Jesus lives there? *(prayer, pictures, crucifix on wall, love, forgiveness, joy, healing, etc.)*

The three kings searched for knowledge. They searched for truth and they searched for God. We are like the Wise Men: on the lookout for signs that Jesus lives among us, especially in our homes.

It has been an old custom in our Catholic Church to bless the homes of believers on this feast day. The family gets together under a doorway in the home and the father or mother leads the blessing and marks with a chalk above the doorway 19—— C — M — B *(places this on flannelboard)*. This is the year and these are the initials of the Wise Men—Caspar, Melchior and Balthasar.

For each child we have a piece of chalk and a star with the blessing to use today in the blessing of your home.

As a matter of fact!! This room is our parish's home. Let's bless this house on the Epiphany. *(Takes a piece of chalk and a star with the blessing on it and leaves the room...goes to a doorway..uses the ladder..writes the markings above the door with chalk. Leads the congregation in the house blessing that is on the star)* I think it would be a good idea to leave this star above the door so that the virtues written in the blessing— health, happiness, faith, love, humility, goodness, mercy and peace, all signs of Jesus' life—will grow and blossom in our hearts. *(Tells the children that stars and chalk will be given to them as they return to their seats)*

COMMUNAL PRAYER

PRAYER LEADER

(One king holds an incensor, one holds the incense powder, and the third prepares it, as the prayer leader says,)
According to tradition, one of the gifts brought by the Wise Men was frankincense, a substance which when burned gives off a pleasing odor. It was used in ancient times and is still used in churches today to show honor and respect to whatever or whomever the incense is directed toward. *(Two kings stand aside while the third with*

the incensor blesses everyone. He then joins the other two kings and they walk off.)

READER   The children who brought a book to exchange today may come up after Mass and choose one to take home.

SONG LEADER   "We Three Kings"

A Light in the Darkness

(Third Sunday of the Year—Winter)

Isaiah 8: 23-29; 9: 1-3, 1 Corinthians 1: 10-13, 17, Matthew 4: 12-23

THEME   Jesus keeps God's promise that a "Light will come into the darkness."
We are also to be lights.

PROPS
1. Letters in a prominent place: A Light in the Darkness
2. Also in a prominent place are five black lifesize silhouette figures of people (including child size). A 10″ heart is cut out of the chest area of each of the "people" and an electric candle is taped to the wall inside this heart area. The area is then covered with another piece of black paper, to be removed during the homily. All "people" lights are lit (but cannot be seen) when the celebration begins.
3. In front of the room is a black box with a window cut out of each side panel. The window is covered with cellophane. An electric candle is placed inside. It will be lit during the Lesson.
4. A large map of Palestine (purchased or drawn with the help of a opaque projector) with the areas of the tribes of Napthali and Zebulun labeled (their land was Northern Israel) is displayed on an easel. A black construction paper cloud covers this area during pre-gospel discussion.
5. Names "Isaiah" and "Prophecy" on rectangular pieces of paper, used in pre-gospel discussion
6. Handouts are 8″ silhouette of children with the typed insert: I can reform my life by _____,

_____, _____.

PERSONNEL
1. Presenter
2. Prayer leader
3. Song leader
4. Reader

GREETING

PRESENTER   Today Jesus proclaims "The Kingdom of God is at hand."

Welcome. How appropriate that the Scriptures speak of "A light in the darkness" when the winter days are short and the nights so long. We need light, the light of the Lord especially.

OPENING PRAYER

PRAYER LEADER   Lord Jesus, sometimes I am afraid. I ask myself, "Am I useful? Am I good? Am I loved?" You are my strength. Sometimes I lose direction. I'm confused. It's hard to make decisions. You are my guide. Lord Jesus, sometimes I don't care. I'm apathetic. I feel things won't change. Lord, be my hope.

FIRST READING

READER   Isaiah 8:23-29; 9: 1-3

SONG LEADER   "New Hope" (*Hi God II*)

GOSPEL

PRESENTER   Come up front, children. When someone promises us something, we wait to see if that promise is kept, don't we? In our first reading today, we heard a messenger from God making a promise. His name was Isaiah (*refers to the name attached to the pulpit*). A long time ago God's people, the Israelites, were very sad because things weren't going well for them. They fell away from God; and to make matters worse a powerful army conquered their land, the land of Napthali and Zebulun. Those are strange names. Can you say them? (*Repeats with the children "Napthali" and "Zebulun."*) Things were truly dark and dreary for these people. (*Places the black cloud over this area on the map.*) Isaiah gave them hope. He gave them a promise. He said that a light will come to brighten their lives.

Well, 700 years later that light came. And St. Matthew, a writer of the New Testament, wants us to be sure we know that when Jesus came the promise was kept! Let's listen to the Gospel of St. Matthew (4:12-17).

LESSON

PRESENTER   Is anyone here afraid of the dark? (*Looks for responses*) In the dark we can't see what's around us. Most of hate to walk in the dark because we may stumble and fall. Sometimes when you go to sleep your Mom or Dad will put on a little night light. And that little light can take away the fear. Jesus is like that light. He came to take away our fear—to guide us in the direction we should go—to give us hope.

See this black box? The pretty window cannot be seen until we light the candle within. *(Plugs in the light)* Jesus says, Reform your lives. Change your lives. Become lights like me—then your world will not be dark. But how do we reform? How do we become lights? Any suggestions? *(Follow God's rules, give up our bad habits, be helpful, read scripture. As the children offer the "reforming suggestions," ask them one by one to change the people on the back wall. This is done best if pre-planned. Children will know how to remove the chest cover, exposing the lit candle.)*

Now our people are people of light. If each of us could be such a light, how could our world remain dark? Each of us must decide for ourselves how our lives need to be changed. You will be given a small paper person. Take a few minutes today and write (or have your parents write) the ways you can reform your lives and become lights. Your parents too will think about the ways God calls them to change. Keep this little person around as a reminder to see how you're doing. *(Paper people are passed out and the children return to their seats)*

COMMUNAL PRAYER

PRAYER LEADER   Please respond, "Lord, hear our prayer."

May our homes be truly Christian—places of support, forgiveness and expressions of love, we pray to the Lord...Lord, hear our prayer.

May we as Christian Americans be committed to our role as peacemakers among the nations, we pray to the Lord...Lord, hear our prayer.

Help us to work in our local communities and overseas to shed light on the darkness of poverty, social injustice, disease and hunger, we pray to the Lord...Lord, hear our prayer.

SONG LEADER   "We Are the Children of the Lord" *(Hi God II)*

As Our Father Loves

(Seventh Sunday of the Year—Winter)

Leviticus 19: 1-2, 17-18, 1 Corinthians 3: 16-23, Matthew 5: 38-48

THEME Love as our Father loves

PROPS
1. Large balance scales made to stand 4½ feet high. Use a 2×4 held upright with a stand (perhaps a Christmas tree stand). A large bolt is screwed through the top of the 2×4. A piece of wood 3 feet × 2 feet × ½ foot is used as a cross bar. A hole a bit larger than the width of the bolt is drilled through the center of this piece so the crossbars can rotate easily but not too sloppily. Medium sized disposable pizza pans are used for each side of the scale. Three pieces of cording or rope about 18 inches long fastened at three equidistant places are placed under pans and knotted together at top. Each pan is draped over the ends of the cross bar (tack or tape so they won't slide off).
2. In a place where everyone will be able to see, place a 4×4 foot white heart made of contact paper. On the heart is attached smaller red contact paper hearts which will be used as handouts. "A Chi Rho" or the words "Christ Love" is written on these smaller hearts. A half of the sticky portion is exposed to fasten onto the larger heart and to adhere to the children's clothing when applied.
3. Large (1 ½ feet wide) double faced red paper heart stapled and stuffed with one pound of beans. One side is lettered "God's Love, and the other side should say "Caring for our well being"
4. A ten inch wide heart made as above but stuffed with 3 pounds of beans. The words "Our love" are written on one side and "caring for another's well-being" on the other side.
5. Six small red hearts (5 inches wide) filled with ½ pound of beans in each—no lettering
6. Small grey or brown hearts that say "Even Steven" made out of contact paper to be placed on each child as they come to church
7. Five pound weight and 3 pounds of potatoes in a peck basket to be used during the homily. Also have extra potatoes on hand to add to the scale.
8. Sign that says "Justice" to be hung on scale
9. Box with a figure of a person and the words "Two Hours" written on it

PERSONNEL	1. Presenter
	2. Prayer leader
	3. Song leader
	4. Reader

GREETING

PRESENTER Today we celebrate loving as our Father loves us. Welcome. I see we are all wearing hearts that say "Even Steven." I wonder what that means? Perhaps we will learn from today's scripture reading.

OPENING PRAYER

PRAYER LEADER For those times when we only want to take and not give.
For those times when people hurt us and we want to hurt them back.
For those times when we're kind only when others are kind to us, we ask your mercy, Lord.

FIRST READING

READER Leviticus 19: 1-2, 17-18

SONG LEADER "Our God is A God of Love" *(Hi God II)*

GOSPEL DISCUSSION

PRESENTER Before we listen to our gospel, I would like to talk a bit about this apparatus here. Can anyone tell what it is? (Motioning to scales.) Right! This is a form of balance scales. It can be used for weighing objects. If we would like to weigh 5 pounds of potatoes, we would put a 5 pound weight on this side, *(Places wrapped 5 pound bag of flour on the left side)* and our potatoes on this side *(places about 3 pounds of potatoes in a peck basket on the right side)*. We would keep adding potatoes until the scales would balance, like this. *(Adds potatoes until even)*

A scale like this is used as a symbol of law and justice. *(Places sign saying Justice on the cross bar)* During Jesus' time and also today there are many laws governing people's behavior. For instance if you would hire a person to work in your store for $4.00 per hour and he worked for 2 hours *(removes the contents of scales first, then places a box with a figure of a person and words "2 Hours" on the left side and a box with $8.00 written on it on the right)* how much would you owe him if you are fair? *(response)* $8.00? Right! Fair is Fair—Even Steven.

The people of Jesus' time (and we too) like to use this balance scale justice method for everything. But Jesus tells us in this gospel about something very important that should not be placed on the justice scale. Listen carefully and find out what is is.

GOSPEL

PRESENTER   Matthew 5: 38-48

LESSON

PRESENTER   That was the gospel of the Lord. What was Jesus speaking of in this gospel? *(response)* Yes, loving like his heavenly Father loves. Let's not confuse love with feeling good about someone or wanting to be with them. Let's consider love as "caring for another's well being"—wanting to do what's best for them. God's love is like this. *(Holds up the large paper heart stuffed with one pound of beans. The front is lettered, "Caring for our well being." Places the heart on the left hand side of the scale.)* No matter how much we do or say, our love could never equal God's love. *(Presses down on the right side to try to balance the scale.)* Would God make his love for us less because we don't even it out? No. His love is generously given, not weighed out.

Jesus wants us to love in the same way. Let's consider our love for other people. *(Removes God's heart and replaces it with a 3 pound heart lettered "Our Love")* It's easy to love, to care for another's well being when they invite us to dinner *(places ½ pound hearts in the right side pan as loving acts are mentioned)*, send us birthday cards, or Christmas gifts, or give us compliments, drive us to places we need to go, give us hugs and kisses *(scales almost balance)*. See, it's almost just, isn't it? Even people who don't believe in God love like this. But what about those people who don't seem to love back *(removes the small hearts from the pan)*, who get on our nerves, or who perhaps have hurt us. Maybe they made fun of us. *(Pause)* And what about those people who go against what we believe—they may cheat at games or tests, they may steal, or take drugs. Some people may even kill our countrymen—the gospel calls them enemies. We may not like them, or feel good about them, but do we take away our love, our "caring for their well being" because the balance is gone?

No, Jesus expects more of his followers. He said you must love perfectly as My Father loves perfectly. Good or bad, we are all his children. We are brothers and sisters to each other.

Do you think you can try to love like this? To truly care for each other? *(Yes)* If so, raise your right hand and say "I promise." *(say together)* If you promised, you may exchange your "even-Steven" hearts for the heart of a Christian on the back wall. When you get your new heart, you may return to your seats.

COMMUNAL PRAYER

PRAYER LEADER Please respond, "Lord teach us to love."

Lord, it is difficult to love as you want us too. Open our eyes so that we may see our brothers and sisters as you see them, we pray to the Lord…Lord, teach us to love."

Help us as a parish never to forget our duty to care for the well being of the imprisoned, those in drug rehabilitation, those plagued by alcholism,we pray to the Lord…"Lord, teach us to love."

Help us as a nation to strive for understanding compassion and openness in working with countries. Let us not label another country as our enemy,we pray to the Lord…"Lord, teach us to love."

SONG LEADER "This is My Commandment" *(Hi God II)*

No Woe, No Glow

(Second Sunday of Lent—Spring)

Genesis 12: 1-4, 2 Timothy 1: 8-10, Matthew 17: 1-9

THEME   Becoming like Jesus is wonderful but it is not easy.

PROPS
1. Three colored pictures depicting the gospel story will be held by 3 children and set on the easel as Presenter reads the gospel.
2. Willie the Worm puppets made from two bright colors of fake fur (we used orange and green). To make Willie, cut 6″ wide strips 16″ long. You will need three of each color. Sew these together alternating colors. Closing tail end, sew into a tube 2/3 of the way down. Leave a hole for Presenter's arm: 1/3 hangs behind arm. The face is 2 layers of white netting cut into a 10 inch circle. Glue or sew into front opening, gathering as you go. Glue black felt eyes onto the netting. Black pipe cleaner is twisted through the netting to make a long antenna. A flashlight is hand-held and goes into Willie's head.
3. Flannelboard and easel. A cardboard mountain approximately 4 feet high placed on the easel—a blue sky in the background.
4. Sign saying "Glow Mountain"
5. Sign saying "3 miles to Glow Mountain"
6. Old worm on Glow Mountain
7. Sign saying, "Go Willie, Go!"
8. Sign saying, "No Woe, No Glow"
9. Sign saying, "No Cross, No Gloss"
10. Sign saying, "No Pain, No Gain"
11. Replicas of Willie's signs to give to the children after the Lesson. (Use small pieces of construction paper with popcycle sticks for sign handouts.)
12. Stool

PERSONNEL
1. Presenter
2. Prayer leader
3. Song leader
4. Reader
5. Children to hold pictures at Gospel
6. Four children to hold up signs during Lesson

GREETING

PRESENTER   Today we celebrate that developing the spirit of Jesus in us is a difficult but worthwhile task. Welcome. We gather today to share Jesus' life, to pray with and for each other, to sing together, to support one another as God's family.

OPENING PRAYER

PRAYER LEADER   Heavenly Father, you have given us Jesus, your Son, to show us the way to live—to be the best we can be. Through his life and his death we have learned that the way is not always easy. With your grace we are able to bear and even overcome hardships in life. Thank you, Father. We will praise you and love you forever through Jesus. Amen.

FIRST READING

READER   St. Paul is writing this letter from a prison in Rome. He gives his friend Timothy encouragement by reminding him of Christ's everlasting life. 2 Timothy 1: 8-10

SONG LEADER   "God Is A Surprise" *(BWYAP)*

GOSPEL
(adapted from Mathew 17: 1-9)

PRESENTER   We have some pictures to help tell our Gospel story today. Would the children like to come up here and sit?

A reading from the Holy Gospel according to Matthew.

Jesus took Peter, James, and his brother John and led them up on a high mountain by themselves. He was changed before their eyes.

(First picture is presented and placed on easel [Jesus glorified - clothes shining]) His face became as dazzling as the sun, his clothes as radiant as light. Suddenly Moses and Elijah appeared to them, talking with Jesus.

(Second picture is presented and placed on easel [Moses and Elijah stand on both sides of Jesus] Second child takes place next to first)
Then Peter said to Jesus, "Lord, how good it is that we are here. With your permission, we will stay here and I will set up three tents, one for you, one for Moses and one for Elijah." He was still speaking when suddenly a bright cloud overshadowed them.

(Third picture is presented and placed on easel [Jesus with cloud above head, apostles covering heads] Third child stands next to second)
Out of the cloud came a voice which said, "This is my beloved Son on whom my favor rests. Listen to him." When they looked up they didn't see anyone but Jesus.

As they were coming down the mountainside, Jesus commanded them, "Do not tell anyone of the vision until the Son of Man rises from the dead."

The disciples discussed among themselves what "rising from the dead" could mean.—This is the gospel of the Lord.

(Picture holders take pictures with them when they leave. A child places sign "Glow Mountain" on the mountain. This child also places a cardboard Old Worm at side of easel, and "3 miles to Glow Mountain" sign in place. Another places a stool behind easel. Selected children will bring their signs up with them.)

LESSON

PRIEST   If you listened carefully to the reading, you found that even the disciples didn't quite understand what "to rise from the dead" meant. It was only after Jesus did die and rise from the dead that they began to understand.

This Gospel reminds me of an old friend of mine—(put on puppet) Willie the worm. Willie also wanted to know about dying and rising, only he didn't call it that. He called it "growing to glow." He also had to go to a mountain to find out what it meant. The story goes like this:

"Growing To Glow"
by Sr. Mary Chupein, S.F.C.C.

Once upon a time there was a worm named Willie. Willie had one ambition in life, and that was to "glow." He didn't know where he got the notion, but he knew he wanted this more than anything on earth. Willie spent his days dreaming and his nights nightdreaming about what it would be like to be a "worm aglow." But all his daydreaming did nothing to light the way. He decided right then and there that he was going to find out. He decided to set out to find someone who could help him grow to glow.

On the third day of his travels, he came upon a sign: "3 miles to Glow Mountain." *(Willie looks at sign)* Days later, a tired, hungry, dirty Willie squirmed to a stop. Glow Mountain towered high above his small worm self. *(Willie is at base of mountain looking up)* At the foot of the mountain sat an old wrinkled worm with eyes that glowed like neon lights. Willie pulled himself over to the old worm and spoke quickly. *(Willie puts his face next to Old Worm)* "Sir, can you tell me how to Grow to Glow?" "You have come to the right place," blinked the old worm, "For I am the keeper of the secret of Glow Mountain. Are you sure you want to know the secret? Well, then, listen carefully," said the secret keeper solemnly. "If you want to know the secret of Glow Mountain, climb to the top."

"You mean that's the secret?" Willie said and shook his head. He did not understand. "You mean all I have to do is climb to the top of the mountain if I want to grow to glow?" The wise old worm simply nodded and then he was gone. *(Old worm is removed from the mountain)*

Willie struggled within himself. Should he climb or shouldn't he? "Oh, dear" said Willie, "if only I knew what to do." *(Child holds up first sign saying "Go, Willie, Go!" Encourage the children to repeat this two or three times as a cheer.)*

Willie looked to the top of the mountain. Suddenly he felt something happen inside him. He felt warm and full of courage. So with his worm head held high, Willie began to climb the mountain. The way was steep and difficult, but Willie knew he could make it! *(Presenter walks behind mountain and stands on stool so that Willie gets to the top)* Then one day he reached the top, and a strange thing happened. He began to grow brighter *(turns on flashlight in head)* and brighter until he was filled with light inside and outside. "So this is what it means to Grow to Glow," sighed a happy Willie. "I think I shall stay here forever." *(Lets him rest on mountain and squirm a little there)* Then something within him said, "Go down, Willie, and tell all the others how to Grow to Glow." "But what shall I tell them?" "You will know," said the voice within him. *(Turns off light inside Willie)*

So Willie began the long trip down the mountain. He had not gone very far when he found a sign. *(Child holds up second sign saying, "No Woe, No Glow." All kids repeat.)* "Strange, "said Willie, but he memorized the message. Slowly, carefully he descended down, down, down. When he reached the halfway point, he found another sign. It read: *(child holds third sign saying, "No Cross, No Gloss." All kids repeat.)* "What does this mean?" asked Willie. He was a bit bewildered by the signs. At last he reached the bottom and, you guessed it, another sign. *(Child holds up fourth sign saying, "No Pain, No Gain." All kids repeat.)*

Willie sat and pondered the last three signs. Somehow he knew that they were the clue to the secret of glowing. One could not stay on the mountain top. There must be a way of glowing down here, mused Willie. Willie thought and thought. The glow inside grew and grew and he knew what he had to do. *(Turns on light inside Willie.)*

The way would not be easy. The worm world in which he lived believed in the "easy life"—looking out for #1—plenty of leisure, food, and good times. No mention of "pain, woe, or cross." Maybe his friends would think him weird teaching worms how to grow to glow.

Yet Willie knew he carried a glow within, and that would light his way. He began his journey around the world, and to this day he can be heard saying in his loudest worm voice, "What does it matter if there is pain and woe? It's worth it all growing to glow!!" *(The End)*

What do you think these signs mean? *(response)*
What does "growing to glow" mean to you? *(response)*

I think there's a light—the spirit of God—in each of us that wants to shine, to "glow." It can be a wonderful warm brilliance. Working for others, listening to them, having patience, forgiving when you've been hurt—that's pain, woe, a cross.

Lent is a good time to grow to glow by doing some of the difficult tasks: chores, helping a friend at school, talking politely to your sisters and brothers, reading them a book.

We've made a little replica of Willie's signs for you. How about taking one home with you to remember Jesus' and Willie's message. *(Signs are passed out to children)* You can now return to your seats.

COMMUNAL PRAYER

PRAYER LEADER   Today's response is "Lord, we know you are listening."

That all sick people will get well, and for the poor, the hungry, the handicapped, we pray to the Lord...Lord, we know you are listening.

For those who are out of work, we pray to the Lord...Lord, we know you are listening.

For all peoples fighting in wars all over this world, that there be more peace on earth, we pray...Lord, we know you are listening.

SONG LEADER   "Abba Father" (On the Carey Landry album of the same name)

Living Water

(Third Sunday of Lent—Spring)

Exodus 17, 3-7, Romans, 1-2, 5-8, John 4, 5-15, 19-26, 39, 40-42

THEME Whoever drinks this water I give him will never be thirsty.

PROPS
1. People to serve drinks of ice water from a cloth covered table in front
2. Two half-filled pitchers of water from the entrance procession to be poured into the baptismal font
3. Presenter will take a drink of water after the entrance procession.
4. A movable baptismal to serve as well during the dramatic reading of the gospel. If your baptismal font is not movable, place a piece of cardboard around a clothes basket. Use a sponge dipped in white latex paint, and sponge rectangles onto the cardboard to look like bricks. This will make the well look authentic.
5. Chair and a bucket to be used during the gospel narrative
6. Two plants—one withered and the other healthy
7. Small flats of seedlings for children to "nourish"

PERSONNEL
1. Presenter
2. Prayer leader
3. Song leader
4. Reader
5. Two children to carry water
6. Children to play the parts of Jesus, woman at the well

GREETING

PRESENTER Jesus is our life-giving water. Today we have pitchers of ice water here in front. If anyone would like a refreshing glass of water, please come up now.

Welcome. It looks like someone left a drink of water for me. *(Takes a drink)* Oh, that tastes good! How many of you had a drink of water today? *(Show of hands)* Refreshing wasn't it?

In the scriptures today, Jesus also talks about water. He says he is our life-giving water.

OPENING PRAYER

PRAYER LEADER   God, our Father, you offer us life eternal through your son, Jesus. Help us, like the Samaritan woman, to recognize his call. Through your son, we offer thanks and praise forever and ever. Amen.

FIRST READING

READER   Exodus 17: 3-7

SONG LEADER   "Wonder of Creation" (BWYAP)

GOSPEL DRAMATIZATION
(adapted from John 4: 5-15, 19-26, 39, 40-42)

(Jesus sits on a chair near the "well." Woman carries a bucket and stands next to him.)

PRESENTER   A reading from the Holy Gospel according to John.

Jesus was passing through a Samaritan town called Shechem and, feeling tired, sat down by Jacob's well to rest. It was mid-day, and very hot. He was alone because his disciples had gone into the town to buy food. A Samaritan woman come to draw water and Jesus said to her,

JESUS   Would you give me a drink of water, please.

PRESENTER   Jews did not associate with Samaritans, so the woman, being surprised, said,

WOMAN   You are a Jew. How can you ask me, a Samaritan and a woman, for a drink?

PRESENTER   Jesus replied,

JESUS   If only you recognized God's gift, and who it is that is asking you for a drink, you would have asked him for a drink instead, and he would have given you living water.

WOMAN   Sir, you don't have a bucket and this well is deep. Where do you expect to get this flowing water? Surely you don't pretend to be greater than our ancestor Jacob, who gave us this well?

PRESENTER   Jesus replied,

JESUS	Everyone who drinks this water will be thirsty again. But whoever drinks the water I give him will never be thirsty.
PRESENTER	The woman, still not understanding, said,
WOMAN	Give me this water, sir, so that I won't grow thirsty and have to keep coming here to draw water. I can see you are a prophet. Our ancestors worshipped on this mountain, but you people claim that Jerusalem is the place where men ought to worship God.
PRESENTER	Jesus told her,
JESUS	Believe me woman, an hour is coming when you will worship the Father neither on this mountain or in Jerusalem. You people worship what you do not understand, while we understand what we worship; after all, salvation is from the Jews.
WOMAN	I know there is a messiah coming. When he comes, he will explain everything.
PRESENTER	Jesus replied,
JESUS	I who am speaking to you; I am the one.
PRESENTER	This is the gospel of the Lord.

LESSON

PRESENTER	Sometimes the meaning of the gospel is hard to understand. We have just seen Jesus and the Samaritan woman at the well. Let's talk about that.
	Jesus mentioned the importance of water. All living things need water. Without it, we can't live. Everybody knows this. Here's something that isn't getting enough water. *(Picks up withered plant. Comments on drooping.)*
	Now let's look over here at a healthy, beautiful plant. Because it has received enough water, it can grow and bloom.
	You children will also have a chance to watch a plant of your own grow and bloom. After this celebration we will pass out flower seeds. The seeds will need careful watering so you can enjoy the plants as they grow.

Sometimes we experience a water shortage. The lack of enough water can cause grave problems that affect us all in many areas: industry, farming, our everyday lives. And only when we lack it do we realize how valuable it is.

Water can be refreshing, too. Imagine a sweltering summer day, a day when just sitting in the shade makes you sweat. What really makes you feel good? Who can tell me? (*Swimming, lemonade, etc.*) Sometimes nothing can quench your thirst more than a tall glass of ice water.

Our gospel today tells us there is something even more refreshing than water. God's living water—God's grace. Through God's grace. Through God's grace our lives can be renewed. Christ is the well of water and we are the "waterers." When we allow his grace to work through us, we have the ability to refresh, nourish, and support each other. When we withhold our respect and concern for one another, we cut off an opportunity for growth. We actually cut off the "water supply" to our brothers and sisters. So let's remember to be good "waterers" for Jesus. Let us nourish each other as we will water these seeds. (*Seeds or seedlings are passed out.*)

COMMUNAL PRAYER

PRAYER LEADER   Our response today will be "Lord, hear our prayer."

For the poor and starving people in our world let us pray to the Lord...Lord, hear our prayer.

For the sick and suffering let us pray to the Lord...Lord, hear our prayer.

Lord, help us to treat others as we would like to be treated, let us pray to the Lord...Lord, hear our prayer.

SONG LEADER   "Bloom Where You Are Planted" (*BWYAP*)

Color Our World

(Easter—Spring)

Acts 10: 34, 37-43, Colossians 3: 1-4, John 20: 1-9

THEME   Color our world with Easter joy!

PROPS
1. Two bare trees with some paper leaves attached
2. Cardboard tomb (use large paint-dipped sponge to simulate brick design)
3. Plastic eggs to decorate the trees
4. Paint-pallets and brushes given to each child when they come up for the Lesson (actually 5 inch poster board ovals with various colored spots to resemble artist pallets)
5. Paper Alleluia signs to be handed out after the Lesson
6. Cardboard sun on a stick
7. Basket for Mary Magdalene
8. Baskets to hold the paint-pallets and brushes
9. White burial clothes
10. Large Alleluia letters—each on a separate piece of large white cardboard
11. Yellow A's, Red and Blue L's, Pink E, Green U, and Violet I the same size as the white cardboard letters
12. Easter flowers
13. Different colored construction paper flowers, with tape roll on back

PERSONNEL
1. Narrators will be the Presenter and two children as trees
2. Prayer leader
3. Song leader
4. Reader
5. Three child actors
6. Eight children to hang up Alleluia letters
7. Twelve or more children to hang the colors on the Alleluia
8. Someone familiar with sign language to sign the creed.

GREETING

PRESENTER   Easter greetings to all of you, my family! Our colorful church decorations, our spring clothes and smiles all show that a change has taken place. We are born anew—Jesus is alive!

Let us bow our heads and think about our new life a moment (*pauses about 10 seconds.*)

OPENING PRAYER

PRAYER LEADER   Heavenly Father, how happy we are today! We thank you for giving us Jesus, your Son, who lived for us, died for us and now is raised in glory. We thank you for giving us a share in that life. We will always thank you for ever and ever. Amen

FIRST READING

READER   Acts 10: 34, 37-43

SONG LEADER   "Alleluia-Round" (*CTTWS*)

DANCERS   Eight children, each holding an Alleluia letter, skip into the room and place the letters in order in a prominent place.

GOSPEL DRAMATIZATION

(Adapted from John 20: 1-9)

PRESENTER   *Two trees are situated on either side of the tomb. A cardboard sun on a stick is lying on the floor behind the tomb.* Come, let us go to the cemetery outside Jerusalem where Jesus was buried. There we will hear our gospel story. (*Presenter stands behind one tree*)

SYCAMORE   Olive, Olive, are you up yet?

OLIVE   Up do you ask? (*stretching arms and yawning*) Oh, these aching limbs. I don't think I had but a few minutes of sleep last night.

SYCAMORE   No wonder, who can sleep with all the commotion. So many Roman soldiers standing guard over this tomb. They were talking all night.

OLIVE   In all my eighty years in this cemetery, this old olive tree has never seen such as this before. (*pause*) Sycamore, remember the man they placed in here on Friday?

SYCAMORE   The man called "Jesus"?

OLIVE   Yes, "Jesus." Sycamore, didn't his people love him, so tenderly did they wrap him in the shroud.

SYCAMORE	Yes, I saw. (*pause*) I wanted to say then, Olive, but I felt foolish: that dead man was special. I felt a power from him, a strength.
OLIVE	Yes, odd you should say that, I felt it too. (*pause*) Oh look, the sun is rising (*a child behind the tomb raises the sun*). Sycamore, why is the stone door moved? No one is here!
SYCAMORE	Shhh—someone is coming! (*Sycamore and Olive crouch down and in a lower voice say*) A woman—I remember her. She was here when they buried Jesus. (*Mary Magdalene carrying her basket walks sadly up to the tomb. She sees the open door, acts frightened, runs off down an aisle to get apostles.*)
PRESENTER	Early in the morning on the first day of the week, while it was still dark, Mary Magdalene was walking to the tomb.
OLIVE	She's running away! Something scared her!
PRESENTER	When she came to Jesus' tomb, she saw that the stone door had been moved away. So Mary ran off to Simon and Peter and the other disciple and told them, "The Lord has been taken from the tomb! We don't know where they have put him!" Peter and the other disciple ran on their way to the tomb. They ran side by side.
SYCAMORE	Look she is bringing two men back with her!
	(*John and Mary sit or kneel down while Peter looks into tomb and picks up the burial clothes. Peter stands up and shows the clothes to Mary, James enters tomb, then comes out and stands next to Peter.*)
PRESENTER	The disciple reached the tomb first. He did not enter but bent down to peer in. He saw the wrappings laying on the ground. Soon Simon Peter came along behind him and entered the tomb.
	Peter saw the wrappings on the ground and saw the piece of cloth which had covered Jesus' head, not lying with the wrappings, but rolled up in a place by itself. Then the disciple who had arrived first at the tomb went in. He saw and believed.
PETER	These are his burial clothes. He's not here. He's risen! Let's tell the others. (*Peter, Mary and John run off*)
SYCAMORE	(*waits for stillness*) Olive, I don't understand; I'm but an old tree, but I feel what has happened here will change the whole world.
PRESENTER	This is the gospel of the Lord.

PRESENTER   Now will the children please come to the front and help us talk about the good news we have just heard. As you come up, please pick up one of the gifts in the baskets, and then have a seat on the floor.

What was in the packet you just picked up? Paint-pallets! Good idea! Can you tell me who does a lot of painting at Easter time? (*response*) The Easter Bunny paints. He has lots of eggs to decorate.

I think our Alleluia sign here needs some Easter color, don't you? What does *Alleluia* mean? Does anyone remember? (*waits*) It means "Praise to God!" Let's proclaim this "Praise to God!" (*All together.*) Can you do it louder? Let's make our Praise to God word colorful. What color shall we make the A's? How about yellow! With our imagination and some help, I bet we can make the A's yellow. Ready. Raise your brushes. Dab the yellow and begin.

SONG LEADER   "Color the World with Song" (*CTWWS*) (*While they are singing six children will get up and adhere yellow A letters over the white ones. Singing continues as the "coloring" proceeds.*)

PRESENTER   Good job! I knew we could do it. Let's try that with the L's. What color? Blue? Raise your brushes painters! (*Six more children will adhere red and blue paper to the L's*)

PRESENTER   Now for the rest of the colors. A bit of pink, green and violet! Ready Painters! (*The rest of the letters are similarly "colored"*)

PRESENTER   There, it's done! See how we people who believe in Easter, who believe that Jesus is alive, can color the whole world just like we did this *Alleluia*. Not only with paints, but with Easter joy, hope, and forgiveness. If we believe.

Put down your pallets and brushes for a moment. Sign language is difficult for me, but I learned a new sign that I want to share with you. It's "believe." (*Points index finger to forehead, and then holds hands together, right hand over left.*) I think it's a good sign. It's saying that you take a thought and hold on to it. Do it with me, "We Believe."

Easter joy, hope, and forgiveness do color the world and make it a better place. We are the painters. If we believe.

Children, when you leave today, you can pick up an Easter sign to paint at home. With this you can begin to color your world.

PRAYER LEADER   Our response today will be "Risen Lord, hear us."

That we may be the Christ-like painters and make our world a more peaceful and hopeful place, we pray to the Lord...Risen Lord, hear us.

That we may truly keep the Good News of God in our homes. That Scripture be shared and revered there, we pray to the Lord...Risen Lord, hear us.

We thank God and ask his blessing upon everyone here today and especially for those who lead us in your way, we pray to the Lord...Risen Lord, hear us.

SONG LEADER   "Jesus, Wonder of Creation" (BWYAP)

Jesus Lives

(Easter—Spring)

Acts 10: 34, 37-43, Colossians 3: 1-4, John 20: 1-9

THEME   We believe Jesus is alive! We celebrate our faith!

PROPS
1. White ribbons to be tied on upper arms of everyone as they arrive
2. Cardboard tomb and trees at front of room (or branches set in plaster)
3. Children have been told the week before Easter to bring a decorated plastic egg or a blown egg to hang on the trees.
4. Small paschal candles (8 inch tapers) to be handed out to the children during the Lesson (painted with acrylic paints)
5. The "new" Alleluia letters are placed on individual sticks and held high during the gospel acclamation.
6. Stations representing Pilate's home, Temple and the cemetery
7. Scarf for Presenter to wear at gospel
8. Basket for Mary Magdalene
9. White robe for the angel
10. White burial clothes

PERSONNEL
1. Presenter
2. Prayer leader
3. Song leader
4. Child actors for the following parts: Guard, Pilate, Chief Priest, Elder, Angel, Mary Magdalene and Woman, Peter, 10 Disciples, Student

GREETING

PRESENTER   Happy Easter to you all! Today is the greatest holiday of the church. We gather here on this wonderful day as believers! We wear white ribbons on our arms. They are a sign that we share the same Easter faith—the faith we received at Baptism.

Jesus is alive and with us. He will never leave us. He fills us with hope. Let us close our eyes for a moment and thank him for everything he gives us. (*Pauses a full 15 seconds*)

PRAYER LEADER   Heavenly Father, how happy we are today! How happy we are to say "We believe in you, we believe in Jesus!: Thank you for giving us your Son who lived for us, died for us and now is raised in glory. We thank you for giving us a share in that life. Together as one family we will praise you forever and ever. Amen.

FIRST READING
(paraphrased from Acts 10:34, 37-43)

SONG LEADER   "Thank you, Lord" (*Hi God I*)

GOSPEL DRAMATIZATION
Adapted from John 20: 1-9)

(The actor who is playing the part of Peter in the gospel proclaims this reading. It is done as a speech to the people. The stage is arranged as follows: Stage left, Pontius Pilate's house—Stage right, Temple room—Center, cemetery.)

PRESENTER   (*Putting on evangelist's scarf*) For the next few moments I will be St. John. Three other writers—Matthew, Mark, and Luke, have told this same story in their own style.

Now let us go back 1986 years ago. It's Easter morning in Jerusalem. Dawn is breaking. We are at Pontius Pilate's mansion.

SCENE I

GUARD   (*wearing helmut, cape, and breast plate, comes up an aisle calling*) Governor Pilate! Important news...Governor Pilate!

PILATE   (*Steps forward from his station wrapped in a bathrobe, a laurel wreath on his head, rubbing his eyes sleepily*) What is it? What can be so important at this awful early hour?

GUARD   (*Gives a military salute by hitting forearm across chest*) My Lord, the captain of the guards standing watch in the cemetery reports that the Nazarean's tomb is empty!

PILATE   (*More agitated*) What now!! Those lazy louts probably fell asleep or left their posts. (*pauses, thinking*) I thought we were finished with this Jesus problem. Now more trouble.

GUARD   (*Meekly*) Sir, do you think he could have...like he said...been raised from the dead?

PILATE   Have you gone crazy!! You can't understand these Jewish people. Do you know what else this Jesus preached? (*counting on fingers*) That God is his loving father; that there is life everlasting; and that he could forgive sin—all foolishness!! (*pauses, thinking, then determining*) No more!! (*pointing a finger at the guard*) I want a full report on this tomb business before noon today. (*He walks off and guard leaves*)

PRESENTER   At the same time, in another section of Jerusalem, in the council room of the temple, the chief priest and elders have heard the news.

SCENE II

CHIEF PRIEST   (*wearing ornate robes and Bishop's hat*) The tomb empty? It's a trick! That Joseph of Aramathea offered his tomb for Jesus' burial. We should have known he was up to something. They stole his body.

ELDER   (*wearing long ornate tunic and fancy stole*) This will stir the people up again. (*wringing his hands, worried*) He had quite a following, you know.

CHIEF PRIEST   (*wagging a finger at elder*) And don't you forget—that's just what he was: a false prophet! You'll see—in a few days this will all die down and be forgotten. (*both exit*)

(*Mary Magdalene and another woman walk up to the tomb and act surprised*)

PRESENTER   The gospel according to St. John. Early in the morning on the first day of the week, while it was still dark, Mary Magdalene was walking to the tomb. (*Mary walks toward tomb, picking up flowers on the way, adding them to her basket*) When she came to Jesus' tomb, she saw that the stone door had been moved away. (*Mary looks at door opening cautiously and with fear, drops the basket and runs off*)

So Mary ran off to Simon Peter and the other disciple and told them, "The Lord has been taken from the tomb! We don't know where they have put him!" (*Peter and John begin running up to tomb. Peter holds up while John keeps running*) Peter and the other disciple ran on their way to the tomb. They ran side by side. The disciple reached the tomb first. (*John kneels in front of tomb, peering in*) He did not enter but bent down to peer in.

Soon Simon Peter came along behind him and entered the tomb. (*Peter enters door of tomb*) Peter saw the wrappings on the ground and saw the piece of cloth which had covered Jesus' head not lying with

49

the wrappings but rolled up in a place by itself. Then the disciple who had arrived first at the tomb went in. (*After Peter exits, James enters tomb*) He saw and believed.

PETER   (*standing, holding up the white wrappings*) I don't understand all of this but *I* believe! He is raised! Let us tell all of his followers Jesus is alive! (*Peter, Mary Magdalene, and John walk down the aisle saying to the persons on the ends of the rows, "He's alive! Pass it on!"*)

PRESENTER   (*When message-passing is done*) This is the gospel of our Lord Jesus Christ.

LESSON

PRESENTER   Our gospel story has to do with believing. Did the Roman guard and Pilate believe that Jesus rose from the dead? (*response, No!*) Did the Pharisees and religious leaders believe that Jesus was alive? (*No*) Did Jesus' friends, Peter, James, Mary Magdalene and apostles believe? (*Yes!*) And how about you? Do you believe? (*Yes!*) I can't hear. (*waits for response again*) I still can't tell. How about some Faith in Action. All of you children who believe that Jesus arose from the dead on Easter morn and is alive with us now, stand up. Good! You may sit down. I have another question to ask. All children who believe that Jesus teaches us the best way to live, raise both of your hands. Great! Do you believe that Jesus loves you very much? Clap your hands. If you believe that one day you will see Jesus face to face, make this sign language—I (*points to self*) believe (*points to head and then clasps hands*). Good, let's do that again. "I believe."

Our belief is what brings us together here. The white ribbon on your arm is like the white baptismal garment you wore when you were a baby. It's a sign of belief. Our Easter Candle is another sign (*stands near candle*). Every year on this day we begin with a new candle—a sign of Jesus being alive with us. We have little Easter candles for you to use this day. When you receive one, look at the markings on it and we'll talk about what they mean. (*Passes out candles here*) See, here is the year 19—— and the cross with the marks for the wounds Jesus received in his hands, feet, and chest. What do you think this is here? (*points to the water sign*) Water. Why would water be on an Easter Candle? Is water a sign of life? (*response*) Yes, every living thing needs water. In our church we have the waters of baptism poured over your head when you become one of Jesus' followers, so water is especially significant in our religious life.

Bless these Easter candles, Lord. May their use in family prayer and meals unite mothers, fathers, sister, and brothers in your spirit.

PRAYER LEADER   Our response will be "Risen Lord, Hear Us."

That we act like a new people today—happy and kind, filled with your hope, we pray to the Lord...Risen Lord, hear us.

That our faith will grow and grow so that we come closer to you and to your will, we pray to the Lord...Risen Lord, hear us.

We thank you for our Parish family—for every person here who shares their faith with us, especially _____ we pray to the Lord...Risen Lord, hear us.

SONG LEADER   "Signs of New Life" (*Hi God II*)

Living Bread

(Third Sunday of Easter—Spring)

Acts 2: 14, 22-28, 1 Peter 17-21, Luke 24: 13-35

THEME	We are living bread for one another.
PROPS	1. Film strip "Little People's Scripture Stories" episode 10
	2. Projector
	3. Different kinds of breads in a basket
	4. Grain or stalk of wheat, flour, yeast, rising bread dough (frozen stretches nicely) in a bowl, pitcher of water, loaf of baked bread
	5. Dinner rolls for kids with a prayer attached
	6. Table and apron
	7. The prayer, duplicated and put in individual baggies with the dinner roll: "Father, may we be food for one another. May we feed each other compliments, support and forgiveness so that we may be more like your son, Jesus. Amen."
PRESENTER	1. Presenter
	2. Prayer leader
	3. Song leader
	4. Reader
	5. Three children to show their pictures after the Greeting

GREETING

PRESENTER

Today we discover that we are living bread. Welcome. In today's scripture, some of Jesus' followers have a hard time recognizing him. Where do we see Christ in our everyday life?

(At this time three children will show pictures they have drawn which answer the question "I see Jesus when...")

OPENING PRAYER

PRAYER LEADER

Heavenly Father, we thank you for the meals we share every day with our family, for those we love, for the joy of being together, and for giving us your son, Jesus, in this special meal.

FIRST READING

READER	Acts 2,14: 22-28
SONG LEADER	"Friends All Gather Round the Table of the Lord" (*BWYAP*)

GOSPEL

PRESENTER	Today we will hear the word of God by watching and listening to a filmstrip.
	(Filmstrip: "Little People's Scripture Stories," episode 10 can be shown silently while presenter reads the gospel.)

LESSON

PRESENTER	That was a good filmstrip, wasn't it? It's a different way of hearing God's word.

In the story, when did the two men find out that the stranger was Jesus? (*When they ate with him, broke bread*) Jesus broke bread with them. Jesus gives himself to us as bread, right? I wonder why he chose bread—why not a fig, or olives, or cheese? (*rhetorical, no responses at this time*)

Here we have a whole basket of breads: let's take a look at them. Maybe they'll give us a clue as to why Jesus chose bread. (*Picks the basket up and then picks up each of the loaves noting: pumpernickel or black bread [Russian and Polish], Jewish Rye [German], Italian rolls, French bread, white sliced [USA], tortillas, [Mexico, Indian], and pita [Middle Eastern]*) We have all different types of bread from all different countries.

Jesus realized that all people use bread for food, for nourishment. He chose a sign that everyone in the world would know and appreciate.

Have you ever made bread, or seen someone making it? Know what this is? (*Holds up the grain or stalk of wheat*) It must be crushed and made into flour. (*Holds up a bag of flour*) Is flour enough? What else do we need? (*Probably the kids will suggest yeast and water—holds up the package of yeast and water*)

Now we put them all together and we put the dough in a warm place and wait and wait, until it looks like this. (*Shows a bowl of rising dough. Passes it around*) Know what? I think we are like bread, all different, shaped, formed, touched by God. (*Kneads the bread dough on the table*)

We then bake the bread and ta-da!! a beautiful loaf. it's nice looking and it smells good, but it's not food until it is broken and shared. (*Breaks the bread in half*)

Yes, we are meant to be living bread, food for one another. We are to share ourselves, to give each other our time and our talents so that we can grow.

Often during our celebrations in church we receive Jesus in this special bread called the Eucharist. He is the best bread...the best kind of food. And all of us who are of age come again and again to the table to find Jesus here just like the two men found Jesus with them at the table.

As you return to your seats today we have a small dinner roll and a prayer to share with your families reminding you to be bread for one another.

COMMUNAL PRAYER

PRAYER LEADER   Our response today is "Lord, show us your bread of life."

For our friends and family let us pray...Lord, show us your bread of life.

For peace in the world let us pray...Lord, show us your bread of life.

For all those who are sick, may they know the healing of Jesus, let us pray...Lord, show us your bread of life.

For all the unbelievers, that they may see the light, let us pray...Lord, show us your bread of life.

SONG LEADER   "Signs of New Life" (BWYAP)

Our Constant Companion

(Sixth Sunday of Easter—Spring)

Acts 8: 5-8, 14-17, 1 Peter 3: 15-18, John 14: 15-21

THEME   We welcome the Holy Spirit in our lives.

PROPS
1. Three poster-size pictures or banners of doves, flame, and wind to be used in Pre-gospel Discussion. These are carried in entrance procession and then placed in stands.
2. The story "The Wind and the Dwarfs," by Max Odorff to be used in the homily as a narration
3. Handouts of paper wind symbols with prayer to Holy Spirit imprinted (see Lesson for text). Make these with white tag-board with forms of wind outlined in blue.
4. Sign "Acts of the Apostles" to be attached to a flannelboard or wall before the First Reading

PERSONNEL
1. Presenter
2. Prayer leader
3. Song leader
4. Reader
5. Three children to carry posters or banners which will be placed in stands

GREETING

PRESENTER   Welcome. We gather together again to share our faith. When we pray and eat here together we are aware of God's Spirit. God calls us to look for him also beyond these walls, into every moment of our lives.

OPENING PRAYER

PRAYER LEADER   Lord, too often we are too busy, too involved with ourselves, to see you by our sides. Our ears are filled with chatter, TV and radio commercials, our own complaints; we cannot hear your voice, Jesus. Lord, your creation can touch us with your presence, but we are often too dull to realize.

FIRST READING

READER The First Reading is from the Book of the New Testament called the Acts of the Apostles. (*attaches sign*) This book tells us of the vigorous growth and trials of the Christian community after Jesus' resurrection. Today's reading is from Chapter 8. (*Proclaims Acts of the Apostles 8: 5-8, 14-17*)

SONG LEADER We Believe in the Sun (*Hi God II*)

PRE-GOSPEL DISCUSSION

PRESENTER Let me describe the setting for our gospel. Jesus is sitting around a dinner table with his friends. It is the night before he will die. The apostles are afraid because they know the authorities want Jesus arrested. Jesus loves these frineds very much, and this is his farewell message to them. He promises to send someone after he's gone. Let's listen.

GOSPEL

READER John 14: 15-21

LESSON

PRESENTER That was the gospel of the Lord. So, Jesus told them the Holy Spirit would come to them, and that he would stay with them always.

Do you know what the Holy Spirit looks like? No, I don't either. But we believe in the Holy Spirit and people need signs and symbols to help their faith. So we create pictures. Here are some signs or symbols of the Holy Spirit that we are familiar with. What's this? (*Perhaps they'll say bird*) It's a dove. Here's another one—flame. (*Holds up the third picture*) Can you tell what it is? Wind. In the Old Testament the same Hebrew word is used for both "wind" and "spirit."

I found a little story about the wind that reminds me of the Spirit and us. It's called "The Wind and the Dwarfs."

(*View filmstrip, "The Wind and the Dwarfs," produced by Greggs Educational Service, or read the text from the book written by Max Ororff, St. Mary's College Press, Terrace Heights, Winona, Minn. Use a flannelboard with pictures made from a coloring book or other story book with elves, enlarged with an opaque projector. Or a class of students could illustrate several scenes and have transparencies made. An overhead projector would then be used during the narration.)*

PRESENTER

How did the dwarfs feel about the wind? (*response*) Right, they loved the wind. He was their friend. He was in their work, their play, their song.

Isn't that a beautiful way of seeing the Spirit of God in our lives...that he is in our work, our play, and in our song. That he is our friend?!

The dwarfs were given a choice. They chose to have the wind over material things such as riches, candy and raisins. Things that would pass away.

We too are given a choice. In the gospel Jesus said, "Those people that are caught up in the world, who are not my followers, will not recognize the Spirit."

If we choose to love Jesus by keeping his commandments, keeping him above everything, we will see the Spirit, his Spirit, like the wind and dwarf, will be with us always. He will be our friend.

We have a little prayer for you that you may use when you talk to the Holy Spirit. Let us pray it together now.

Holy Spirit of God, we choose to have you in our lives.
When we walk, Spirit be with us.
When we talk, Spirit be with us.
For you are all around us.
You are in our song.
Amen

COMMUNAL PRAYER

PRAYER LEADER

Let us respond "Come, holy Spirit."

We ask that the Spirit of God grow in our parish so that we may better serve the Lord and do his will, we pray to the Lord...Come, holy Spirit.

May the atmosphere in our homes be God-like, one of peace, concern and good will, we pray to the Lord....Come, holy Spirit.

May we never forget the power of the Spirit present in each of us. May we discover the often hidden gifts God has given. We pray to the Lord....Come, holy Spirit.

SONG LEADER

"Father, We Adore You" (*Hi God I*)

Loving Guardians

(Twenty-Third Sunday of the Year—Fall)

Ezekiel 33: 7-9, Romans 13: 8-10, Matthew 18: 15-20

THEME
: Jesus has commanded that we show genuine love for our neighbors by confronting them kindly with their wrong-doings.

PROPS
: 1. Flannelboard and easel
: 2. Heart shaped badges that the children will exchange with one another. Each child should write his or her name on the heart.
: 3. Signs saying "Ezekiel," "Prophet," and "Guardian"
: 4. Brightly colored pictures for the flannelboard of 1) a tree, 2) three boys, one on the ground and two in a tree, and two girls sitting at their desks, 3) a toy store, 4) a boy with crossed arms, and 5) a boy slipping a model airplane under his jacket

PERSONNEL
: 1. Presenter
: 2. Prayer leader
: 3. Song leader
: 4. Reader

GREETING

PRESENTER
: Today we learn that we are like loving guardians for our brothers and sisters. In today's Scripture, God tells us that we must show genuine love for our neighbors by confronting them when they do wrong. Let us prepare our minds and hearts to accept his words and his life in our celebration of his word.

OPENING PRAYER

PRAYER LEADER
: Heavenly Father, thank you for friends and family who love us enough not only to comfort and praise us but also to point out our mistakes when we've done wrong. Give us the courage to also share this concern for one another. We ask this through Jesus Christ, your son, in union with the Holy Spirit. Amen

READER   Ezekiel 33: 7-9

SONG LEADER   "Thank You God, For Being So Good" (*CTWWS*)

GOSPEL

PRESENTER   Matthew 18: 15-20

LESSON

PRESENTER   Children, would you please come up and sit on the floor here by me. We will talk about the Bible's message today. (*Children come up. A child moves the easel so that the pictures will be accessible.*)

I have some pictures here to help me talk about today's lesson. Pretend that you are a part of this story.

Picture yourself playing with a friend. You're climbing the tree in your backyard. (*Puts up tree, then two boys*) Your little brother is playing with Matchbox cars under the tree. (*Places brother*) You're having a good time, seeing who can reach the furthest branches. Your friend hears his mother calling him. He gets mad and begins to swear. He's done this before. You're upset because you don't want your little brother to hear and pick up these words. How many of you would ask him to stop swearing? How many of you would yell at him? How many would say nothing and just wait for him to leave?

Let's try another picture. You and another friend are shopping at the K-Mart. Your mom said that you two could look around in the toy department there. (*Places picture of toy store*) Your friend, Tom, and you are looking at the model airplanes. (*Places picture of boy with crossed arms*) Tom loves models. You see Tom pick up one and slip it under his jacket. (*Places picture of Tom slipping plane under jacket*) Tom is shoplifting. What would you do? Say something to him? Tell the manager of the store? Say nothing?

Here's our last picture. You are in school having a test (*places picture of girl sitting in desk*), and your friend Susan who sits behind you (*places picture of Susan*) is asking for the answers to some math problems. You don't want her to be mad at you and you know cheating is wrong. What would you do? Talk to the teacher? Talk to Susan? Do nothing?

How do you think God would like us to act in these situations? Would God say, "Mind your own business, you're not your brothers' keepers"? Would he? If you listened to today's readings, you would know the answer.

In today's first reading, God talks to *his* special messenger called a prophet. *(Holds up sign and places it on board)* Can you say that? Prophet. This prophet's name was Ezekiel. *(Holds up sign and places it on board)* That's a hard name. Ezekiel. God told Ezekiel and all of us that we are to be guardians—or keepers of each other's spiritual lives. God used strong language that probably makes us a bit uncomfortable. He said, "Ezekiel, you are the guardian of my people. If your brother is living a bad life and you don't warn him to change his ways, I will hold you responsible." So we are to warn each other if we see we're not living right!

Now does that mean that we're to criticize people, or tattle-tale when they do something wrong? Are we to be angry at them because they're doing wrong and we're doing right? *(response)*

No—in the gospel Jesus says if your brother has sinned, go and speak to him personally. This is not easy but if we ask Jesus, he will help us. So with Jesus' help, what is the best way to act in each of these stories? *(response—that we are to speak gently to our friends, correcting their behavior)*

Helping each other like this is not easy. It takes a lot of courage and a lot of heart. As a reminder of this lesson, let us exchange hearts with one another, so that we have the name of someone we can pray for in a special way and be that person's guardian.

COMMUNAL PRAYER

PRAYER LEADER   Please respond, "Keep love in our hearts, O Lord."

That our homes may not be places of criticism but of loving guidance, let us pray to the Lord...Keep love in our hearts, O Lord.

That our hearts and minds be open not only to your comforting words, Lord, but to those that challenge us, let us pray to the Lord...Keep love in our hearts, O Lord.

That we may have the confidence to use our talents that you have given us, let us pray to the Lord...Keep love in our hearts, O Lord.

SONG LEADER   "This is My Commandment" *(Hi God II)*

Turning Back to God

(Twenty-Sixth Sunday of the Year—Fall)

Ezekiel 18: 25-28, Philippians 2: 1-11, Matthew 21: 28-32

THEME   Things will be okay as long as we return to God.

PROPS
1. Sign hung in prominent place that says "I turn back to you, Lord"
2. Paper pendant faces—smiling on one side, back of head on the other side. These are to be worn around the children's necks. Pass these out to the children as they arrive.

PERSONNEL
1. Presenter
2. Prayer leader
3. Song leader
4. Reader
5. Three children to pantomine gospel. The pantomines wear overalls and big straw hats.

GREETING

PRESENTER   God is constantly turning to us. He calls us to turn to him. Welcome. We are about to sing that God looks on us with love all the time. That's a wonderful thing.

Are the faces that you are wearing facing forward? Yes? Good! Many times our face is not turned toward God.

OPENING PRAYER

PRAYER LEADER   Before we pray, let us close our eyes and sit for a moment, letting go of any bad feeling that we may have brought with us today. (*Waits for at least 30 seconds*)

Heavenly Father, thank you for your never-ending love. Because we are sinful, we often turn our backs to you, yet you always show your face fully to us in Jesus. Through Jesus, your son, we give you thanks and praise for ever and ever.

READER   Ezekiel 18: 25-28

SONG LEADER   "All the Time" (*BWYAP*)

GOSPEL
(adapted from Matthew 21: 28-32)

(The two sons are sitting in the back of the room with their backs to the group. The father is standing in the center of the room. The presenter is at front, narrating.)

PRESENTER   A dramatic reading from the Holy Gospel according to St. Matthew.

Jesus told this story to the religious leaders and priests of the people. Listen to this situation.

There was a man who owned a vineyard. This man had two sons. *(Pause...Man walks to first son)*

He went up to the oldest son and said, "Son, I want you to go out and work in the vineyard today."

(Pause...Man puts hand on son's shoulder, mimes that he wants him to work, hands him a shovel)

The oldest son acted as if he was ready to obey his father. He replied, "I'm on my way, Sir!"

But as soon as his father was out of sight, he put down his tools and ran to play.

(Pause...Oldest son looks over shoulder for the man to leave, mimes leaving tools and skips off)

Then the father went to the second son and asked him to go to the vineyard to work.

(Pause...Father asks and son mimes his unwillingness to work)

The son replied, "No, I don't want to."

(Pause...Son turns his back on the father. Father walks away, head hung, looking sad)

But afterward he was sorry he had said no, and went to do the work.

(Pause...the son turns, looking at floor, feeling bad. Sighs, and picks up the tools and goes off to work)

Jesus asked the priests and leaders which of the two did what the father wanted? They answered, "The second son."

Jesus said strongly, "Let me make it clear—cheaters and sinners are entering the kingdom of God before you people who say you obey all the rules! When John the Baptist came preaching a way to a holy life, you did not believe him, but the cheaters and sinners changed their ways and believed him. Yet even when you saw this you did not repent and believe." This is the gospel of the Lord.

LESSON

PRESENTER   *Points out the words on the sign and asks the kids which of the sons "turned back to his father." Asks them if they ever act like the first son, saying they'll do something, but not doing it [waits for responses]—or like the second son refusing but then feeling sorry.*

Let's play a silent game. You will use your "faces" for this. I'll read a situation and you will answer by turning your paper face forward or backward. Okay, ready?

You're watching TV and your mom calls you to set the table. You call, "Coming, Mom!" but still sit and watch the program. Which way is your face turned?

You were grouchy with your little brother because your dad asked you to take him to the playground. Once you got there, however, you talked nicely, pushed him on the swings, and helped on the slide. Which way is your face turned?

You didn't want to invite Tom to play baseball. He can't bat very well and his catching is even worse. When you saw the look on his face you said, "You wanta play?" Which way is your face turned?

God loves us just the way we are. We don't have to pretend with him. Although we turn from him by being selfish, greedy, disobedient, it is the turning back and saying we're sorry that matters. Let me show you an example.

(Picks two children and poses them so that one child is facing the other's back. Whispers to the one facing the other's back that she should give a cheerful Hi sign to the kid whose back is facing her. Now ask the other if he knows what the greeting is. Of course not. He couldn't see the Hi sign. Thanks the children and dismisses them.)

It's the same with God. He's always greeting us, smiling on us, but we are often turned away. Sometimes we think we're always turning away from God, that our bad habits will never go away. We lose patience. We think we're not good. God doesn't look on us like that. When we turn back to him we experience only patient, never-ending love.

COMMUNAL PRAYER

PRAYER LEADER
To our petitions please respond "Lord, we turn to you."

We ask that all of our families grow closer to you Lord, we pray to the Lord…Lord, we turn to you.

We ask that we never give up trying to be peacemakers at home and school, we pray to the Lord…Lord, we turn to you.

That we, Lord, become your hands and face for one another, we pray to the Lord…Lord, we turn to you.

SONG LEADER
"Like a Sunflower" (BWYAP)

Invitation to a Banquet

(Twenty-Eighth Sunday of the Year—Fall)

Isaiah 25: 6-10, Philippians 4: 12-14; 19-20, Matthew 22: 1-10

THEME
: Our celebration is a true invitation from Jesus. In honor of him we come.

PROPS
: 1. Two poster size party invitations, one to a picnic and one to a party. Purchase invitations or draw them. Blow them up onto hardboard with an opaque or an overhead projector to 18" x 30". On inside write "Please Come. RSVP."
2. One special invitation from Jesus (The picture you use on the invitation could be from a poster. Have a picture of bread and wine on the front and say "Jesus of Nazareth invites you to a banquet in his honor.")
3. Easel
4. Sign that says "You are Invited" put in a prominent place for all to see
5. Bookmarks reflecting theme will be handed out as the children return to seats after the Lesson.
6. If you have access to an overhead projector and screen, appropriate pictures from a filmstrip borrowed from a church's education department can be shown while the Gospel is proclaimed.
7. Or an actor can pantomine the "King's" role while the priest proclaims the Gospel. The "King" (dressed contemporary-style in a suit) sits at a desk writing invitations. A large sign invites his "Special Friends" to a party. His messenger comes, takes smaller invitations from the King, and leaves. The King puts up some crepe paper and a couple of balloons. The messenger returns, acting upset. The King crosses out "special friends" and writes "everyone," puts up a few more balloons, and then he or she exits.

PERSONNEL
: 1. Presenter
2. Prayer leader
3. Song leader
4. Reader

PRESENTER   Good Morning. Banquets, invitations and our response is what our celebration is about today. Welcome. Isn't it great to be invited to a special event? If Jesus invited us we would be sure to say yes, or would we?

OPENING PRAYER

PRAYER LEADER   Lord, you invited me to sit with you awhile to talk to you but I didn't notice. I did notice the latest T.V. program last night and I did notice the neatest jeans jacket I just have to have.

Lord, you invited me to walk for the hungry or volunteer my time for someone who needs me. I didn't hear you inviting me. That wasn't you asking Lord, that was my religion teacher or my mom.

Lord, you invite me to forgive that person who talks about me all the time, who says she can't stand me. I got that invitation, but come on, you can't mean it.

Heavenly Father, you also invite us through your son to your wonderful kingdom. You invite us, not force us to love, to forgive, to celebrate. For these invitations we give you thanks and praise in Jesus' name.

FIRST READING

READER   Isaiah 25: 6-10

SONG LEADER   "Come and Go With Me" (*Hi God II*)

GOSPEL

PRESENTER   Matthew 22: 1-10

LESSON

PRESENTER   Will the children please gather round to share the gospel message. (*Waits for everyone to get settled*) In the gospel that you heard, what was the king planning? (*response*) A wedding party, right! Do you like parties? I do.

The man sent out invitations. Have you ever received a party invitation? (*response*)

I have some invitations here. Let's take a look at them. (*Picks one up and holds it up for all to see; reads it*) This one is an invitation to a picnic. "Please come. RSVP." (*Places this invitation on the easel. Repeats for second invitation*) What does RSVP mean? (*response*) It means you have to tell the host if you are planning to go to the party or not, right? Do you usually say "yes" to an invitation if you are free at the time? (*yes*) What if you think you won't like all the food served there? Will you probably still say "yes"? What if there's a certain game you're not crazy about, will you probably still go? (*yes*)

In today's Bible story did the invited guests say "yes" to the king? (*response*) No. They had excuses why they couldn't come. How did the king feel? (*Hurt, then angry*) Do you think that the boy or girl who sent these invitations would be hurt if everyone said no? Yes, I think so too.

I have another invitation here. (*Takes out Jesus' invitation and places it on the easel*) It says "Jesus of Nazareth invites you to a banquet given in his honor." What do you think that means, banquet? (*Perhaps children will mention the Last Supper, the apostles were invited. Perhaps they will mention Mass, heaven. Accept all possibilities.*)

Let's look inside. It says:

Where:	(Name of your church)
When:	Saturday evenings and Sunday mornings
What for:	Stories, singing, praying and Communion

Yes, Jesus invites us to go to church every Sunday, to listen to his word in the Bible, to sing, pray, and eat. And what have all of you answered? Yes or No? (*response*) I can't hear you. What have you answered? Yes!!

Now be honest with this next question. How many of you really don't like going to church? (*Sees if any respond*) I'm sure many of you find that you don't understand the prayers, or that _____ talks too long, or that it's hard to sit still, and yet—you're here! Your parents bring you in honor of Jesus the host.

Jesus understands how you feel and it's O.K. He's just glad that you're here. I'm sure many of the adults are not crazy about all of the songs, or the homilies, or maybe the prayers lose their meaning after being repeated so often. All Jesus asks of us is to try to celebrate, to find the best in each celebration, to listen to the stories, to answer the prayers, and to sing the songs. Each time it will get a little better and we'll feel more like a family.

Are you glad to be Jesus' guests? Yes? Every week he invites each one of us to come to his banqueting table. There is a song that starts like that. Let us all show how happy we are by singing and using arm motions for one verse of "His Banner Over Me Is Love."

Thank you for listening so well today. You may return to your seats.

COMMUNAL PRAYER

PRAYER LEADER   Please respond "Lord, hear our prayer."

Help us in school and at our jobs to overcome boredom and laziness ...Lord, hear our prayer.

Please help us to be peacemakers in our country, and in our families...Lord, hear our prayer.

One of the hardest things to do in our lives is to let go of grudges. Please help us to forgive...Lord hear our prayer.

That we may look for ways to help the poor and be generous and caring in our lives...Lord, hear our prayer.

SONG LEADER   Leads group in versus two and three of "His Banner Over Me is Love" (Hi God I)

Three Loves in One

(Thirtieth Sunday of the Year—Fall)

Exodus 22: 20-26, 1 Thessaloneans 1: 5-10, Matthew 22: 34-40

THEME
The love of God for us, and our love of ourselves and others are not separated.

PROPS
1. Two large tablets one yard long each depicting five commandments each, put on an easel or hung up. Numbers 1 through 5 are on a strip of paper. Numbers 6 through 10 are on a second strip.
2. The word "Love" hung up or on easel
3. Heavy hemp rope (one inch in diameter, 3 ply and about 10 feet long) carried in by the Presenter and several children
4. Individual 8 inch pieces of thinner rope (baler twine, 3 ply) for each child
5. Roman numerals I, II, and III fifteen inches long, to be added to the tablet during the homily

PERSONNEL
1. Presenter
2. Prayer leader
3. Song leader
4. Reader
5. Children for entrance procession

SONG LEADER
Let us sing "Thank You Lord for Giving Us Life" (Hi God I) as _____ enters. (*Presenter walks to front with 5-6 children, all carrying pieces of rope*)

GREETING

PRESENTER
Today in our gospel we learn the greatest and First Commandment. We are going to celebrate all the times when we can live this First Commandment. Welcome! That was a neat entrance procession. You may be wondering about the rope. We'll find out more about it later. Right now our question is "Whom do you love?" Let's think about that. Do we love God? Do we love ourselves? Do we love our neighbor?

PRAYER LEADER   To prepare for our banquet of love, let's close our eyes. Picture the face of Jesus and imagine him telling you "to love the Lord with your whole heart, whole soul and all your mind." Do we love just enough to get by?" Picture a neighbor's face. We must love them, too. Do you see the face of a neighbor you find hard to love? Picture your own face. Do you love yourself? Have you forgiven yourself the way the Lord forgives you?

FIRST READING

READER   Exodus 22: 20-26

SONG LEADER   "This is My Commandment" (*Hi God II*)

GOSPEL

PRESENTER   Matthew 22: 34-40

LESSON

PRESENTER   (*Invites the children to the front of the room, bringing their rope with them*)

That was the gospel of the Lord. As you can see, we have here a drawing of a tablet like the commandments that Moses had. How many commandments are there? (*Waits for response*) Ten? Right! Can anyone name any of the commandments? (*Waits for response*) Good!

The man talking to Jesus in today's gospel story was a lawyer. Lawyers are very interested in laws. He was kind of testing Jesus. He asked which of these laws was the more important. Instead of mentioning any of these then (walks to the tablet and removes the strip of numbers) what did Jesus say? (*Waits for response but does not repeat aloud*)

He said, "Love God with your whole heart, your whole soul and your whole mind." (*Gives child the Roman number I to put on the empty tablet*)

Then he said "Love your neighbor." (*Gives another child the Roman numeral II to put on second tablet*)

He also said, "Love yourself." (*Gives another child the Roman numeral III*) So, instead of receiving one law, Jesus gave him three laws of love. But if we look and listen closer at what Jesus meant, it really is more like this. (*Puts the II on the I and the III on top of the II*) You cannot separate these loves.

Let's look at this another way. Do you have your pieces of rope? I'll get the big one. (*Bends down and picks up rope, holding one end*) Let's look at our ropes. They're made of hundreds of small fibers formed together to make one strong piece. If we look closer at the ends of our rope we don't see one piece, but how many? (*waits*) Three! Right! So it is with the love Jesus speaks about. The love for God, love for ourselves, love for all other people are intertwined (*shows with twisting of hand*) as one...like this rope.

A love that is given just to God and kept to ourselves is not the best for us. Only when the three loves are together is it a good love of freedom and growth. God wants us to feel good about outselves, to see the best in each other, and to love him together as his children.

So take your ropes and let us make a knot in them, (*makes knot...waits until the children have done it...asks older children to help the little ones*) showing that we bind this three-fold love in our hearts. Perhaps you can place this rope on your kitchen table this week reminding us of this greatest law.

COMMUNAL PRAYER

PRAYER LEADER   To our petitions today please respond, "Lord, help us to love."

We ask that each of us may learn to live our lives according to God's law of Love, we pray, Lord, help us to love.

That we, your children, may grow stronger in your love each day, we pary, Lord, help us to love.

That our love for you may be demonstrated in the love we show for others, we pray...Lord, help us to love.

For everyone to have the strength to live by God's law of love, we pray...Lord, help us to love.

SONG LEADER   "Thank You Lord for Giving Us Life" (*Hi God I*)

Are We Spiritually Healthy?

(Thirty-Second Sunday of the Year—Fall)

Wisdom 6: 12-16, Thessalonians 4: 13-14, Matthew 25: 1-13

THEME
Are we spiritually healthy? Are we preparing ourselves to meet the Lord?

PROPS
1. A decorated doorway that is to be the entrance to the "wedding hall" in the gospel. A four foot long piece of cardboard serves as a bar for the door. Cover the door with brown wrapping paper marked with black magic marker to look like wood. Hang blue and white crepe paper above the door.
2. Cardboard bar to be placed on entrance of the above
3. Book of Wisdom sign displayed at First Reading
4. Stethoscope
5. Physical health check list and spiritual health list (see Lesson) on poster-size signs
6. Large sign—Be Prepared—to be hung in a prominent place
7. Four lanterns with handles, 2 bottles of oil
8. Bags for groom to carry

PERSONNEL
1. Presenter
2. Prayer leader
3. Song leader
4. Reader
5. Four bridesmaids wearing long skirts
6. Groom wearing a tunic with a boat-neck and a sash across one shoulder
7. Guard

GREETING

PRESENTER
Someday we will meet the Lord face to face. Are we ready? Welcome. Our Scriptures today ask us to use our heads to be wise and prepare ourselves to meet God.

PRAYER LEADER   God our wise Father, we seek your wisdom, hoping as we love you we will perceive it. As Wisdom makes her rounds, at dawn or at dusk and in all seasons, we seek her sitting by our gates, and are not disappointed. God, our wise Father, make us free of care.

FIRST READING

READER   Wisdom 6, 12-16
(Announces the source of the reading and then hangs sign "Book of Wisdom" in front of the room, explaining to the children that this book was written for Greek youth to convey that Godly wisdom is more important than human wisdom. The reader uses the word "wisdom" in place of he or she.)

SONG LEADER   "Early in the Morning (CTWWS)

GOSPEL DRAMATIZATION
(adapted from Matthew 25: 1-13)

PRESENTER   *(Gives background information before beginning the Gospel narrative.)* Let us imagine the setting for Jesus' story. A wedding feast is about to begin. It will be a wonderful party that will last all week. Everyone is waiting for the groom to arrive. It's a long journey from his town, and no one knows when he is going to arrive. The bride has chosen ten young women to go out and greet him with their lights when he comes because no one is allowed on the city streets at night without a light.

Jesus told this parable to his disciples:

"The reign of God can be likened to ten bridesmaids who took their torches and went out to welcome the groom."

(Bridesmaids 1, 2, 3, and 4 run up from a side aisle.)

BRIDESMAID 1   Come, let's go.

BRIDESMAID 2   This will be so much fun. I hope he comes soon.

BRIDESMAID 4   I just love weddings!

NARRATOR   Five of the ten were foolish, while the other five were sensible. The foolish ones, in taking their torches, brought no oil along, but the sensible ones brought flasks of oil as well as their torches.
(Bridesmaids to front of room)

BRIDESMAID 1	Didn't you bring any extra fuel?
BRIDESMAID 2	You knew we would be out here all night.
BRIDESMAID 3	I didn't want to bother carrying it. It's so heavy.
BRIDESMAID 4	We'll have enough. He'll be along any minute, you'll see.
NARRATOR	The groom delayed his coming, so they all began to nod, then to fall asleep. (*Pause here for the girls to lay down and pretend to be asleep*) At midnight someone shouted.

(*Guard at back of church shouts*)
The groom is here! Come out and greet him!

NARRATOR	At the outcry all the virgins woke up and got their torches ready. The foolish ones said to the sensible, "Give us some of your oil. Our torches are going out." But the sensible ones replied, "No, there may not be enough for you and us. You had better go to the dealers and buy yourselves some." While they went off to buy it the groom arrived, and the ones who were ready went into the wedding with him. Then the door was barred.

(*During this narration, the girls pantomime. Two girls leave and the other two greet the groom who is walking down the center aisle. They take his bags and lead him to the area of celebration. The guard then places the cardboard bar over the door. When the other two bridesmaids return with oil, they find the door barred and begin pounding.*)

NARRATOR	Later the other bridesmaids came back. "Master, master! Open the door for us," they called. But he answered, "I tell you, I do not know you."

The moral is: keep your eyes open, for you know not the day or the hour.

LESSON

PRESENTER	From our story we can all agree that two of the bridesmaids were foolish, weren't they? They were not prepared. They forgot their oil. They didn't do their job and so they were left out of the party.

We Americans believe in being prepared! We believe in preparing our bodies for health. In school you all have gym class, right? And some of your moms and dads jog or swim or exercise. I like to _____ to stay in shape. All of you here look pretty healthy—how about standing up and showing me how you can touch your toes. Good job! Everybody's pretty limber. How about balance. See if you can stand on one foot for 5 seconds. Good! O.K., sit down now.

(Puts on the stethescope) Let's pretend that I'm a doctor, and we'll fill out this physical health check list. *(Displays poster check list and checks off when hands are raised)*

How many of you have:
1. Measles Shots and Polio Vaccine
2. Vitamins
3. Dental Check-ups and Brushing
4. Nutritious and Balanced Meals
All this is done so that your body is prepared to fight off disease and grow strong so that you can live for a long time.

But what about the part of that you can't see, the part of you that will never die—your soul? Is your soul being prepared for spiritual health? You don't have to raise your hands for this check list, but let's ask and you can think about it. *(Displays poster of spiritual list)*

How many of you:
1. Pray as a family
2. Read Scripture at home
3. Find ways to help someone at least once a day.
4. Sit quietly with God and let him talk to you.
These spiritual health habits prepare you to meet Jesus. If you begin a friendship with Jesus now, when you see him face to face at the end of your life you will know each other. He will say, "Oh Jennifer, or Matthew, I know you! Come into my Father's house!

All of us need help in keeping spiritually healthy. We have to work at it. Today we have a little booklet for you with ideas for your family. You will receive it as you return to your seats.

COMMUNAL PRAYER

PRAYER LEADER   Please respond "Lord hear our prayer."

That doing God's will becomes the most important goal for us, we pray to the Lord...Lord hear our prayer.

That we become spirit-filled and industrious in our jobs at the office, at school, and at home, we pray to the Lord...Lord hear our prayer.

That each of us take time in our daily schedules for personal and family prayer, we pray to the Lord...Lord hear our prayer.

SONG LEADER   "Children of the Lord" *(Hi God II)*

Follow the Leader

(Christct The King—Fall)

READINGS: Ezekiel 34: 11-12, 15-17, 1 Corinthians 15: 20-26, 28, Matthew 25: 31-46

THEME   I will follow you, Lord.

PROPS
1. Shepherd and sheep hung on a back wall or on easel (black silhouettes)
2. Altar cloth with paper words that say "Follow the Leader"
3. Paper footprints leading to the front of the room
4. Paper sheep (with one cotton ball side) handouts. Sheep should have smiling faces and the words, "I will follow Jesus by _____"on the other side. The children will receive these as they arrive. They are to fill in the blank and bring their sheep up with them to place on the wall/easel during the Lesson.
5. Pictures of Jesus washing Peter's feet, and a picture of hands holding bread to be used during the lesson (silhouettes enlarged with opaque projector)

PERSONNEL
1. Presenter
2. Prayer Leader
3. Song Leader
4. Reader
5. Two groups of students who will act as sheep and goats during the gospel narrative

GREETING

PRESENTER   Jesus to be our guide. As a shepherd cares for and leads his sheep, Christ cares for and leads us.

Welcome. Today we celebrate the Feast of Christ the King, and God our Father eagerly shows us the path to his kingdom. It's up to us to follow. Did you see the footprints when you came in? They're making a path for us.

OPENING PRAYER

PRAYER LEADER   Dear God, our Father, we thank you for keeping watch over us. Because we are sinners, we don't always live up to the challenge to be true and loving Christians. Help us to be kind and thoughtful toward one another through your Son, Jesus Christ, our Lord. Amen.

SONG LEADER   "Like a Shepherd" *(Bob Dufford, "A Dwelling Place")*

FIRST READING

READING   Ezekiel 34: 11-12, 15-17

GOSPEL DRAMATIZATION
(adapted from Matthew 25, 31-46)

PRESENTER   A reading from the Holy Gospel according to Matthew . . .

Jesus said to His disciples: When Christ comes in his glory, with all the angels of heaven, he will sit upon his royal throne, and everyone will be assembled before him.

NOTE   *(Presenter is standing back near the wall/easel. Eight "sheep" and "goats" are sitting with their backs to the group near the front of the room.)*

Then he will separate them into two groups, the way a shepherd separates sheep from goats. The sheep he will place on his right side, *(sheep get up and move accordingly)*, and the goats on his left. *(Goats get up.)*

The King will say to those on his right: Come, you have my Father's blessing. You shall have the kingdom that was prepared for you from the beginning of the world!

For I was hungry and you gave me food, I was thirsty and you gave me drink. I was a stranger and you welcomed me, naked and you clothed me. I was ill and you comforted me, in prison and you came to visit me.

SHEEP   Lord, when did we see you hungry and feed you, or see you thirsty and give you drink? When did we welcome you away from home, or clothe you in your nakedness? When did we visit you when you were ill or in prison?

PRESENTER   I assure you, everytime you did this for another person, you did it for me. *(Turns from sheep and faces the goats.)*

But you! Go away from me! I was hungry and you gave me no food, I was thirsty and you gave me no drink. I was away from home and you gave me no welcome, naked and you gave me no clothing. I was ill and in prison and you did not come to comfort me!

GOATS	Lord, when did we see you hungry or thirsty or away from home or naked or ill or in prison and not take care of you?
PRESENTER	I assure you, everytime you did not do this for another person, you did not do it for me. (*Goats turn away from Presenter, heads hanging.*)
	These will go off to eternal punishment, and the just to eternal life.
	This is the gospel of the Lord.

LESSON

PRESENTER	(*Asks children to bring their sheep to the front of the room*)

In the gospel story Jesus talks about God dividing his people into two groups like a shepherd separating the sheep from the goats. What did he say to the sheep? (*They helped people*) How about the goats? (*They did nothing.* What group do you want to be in? (*Wait*) Sheep, of course. I think we all want to be in that group.

Jesus told several stories about shepherds and their sheep. See our picture back here. The people of Galilee where Jesus lived were used to seeing sheep grazing on hills. They knew the shepherds took care of their sheep. They fed them and kept them safe from wild animals. They would see the sheep follow their shepherd home in the evening. Jesus called himself the Good Shepherd. We are his followers.

I see you have small sheep in your hands. On each one it says, "I will follow Jesus by_____." Tell us some ways you follow Jesus. (*Asks several children for examples. Praises the suggestions.*)

I have a picture here that shows how we are to follow Jesus. If we look at it closely we can get an idea of what God wants us to do.

This is a picture of Jesus washing Peter's feet. During Jesus' day, the people wore sandals on the dusty roads, and when they sat down to dinner they would clean their feet and hands. A servant usually washed their feet. Since Jesus was the leader of his friends, isn't it amazing that he is doing the washing? Amazing—yes! Jesus is giving us a lesson. None of us should be too proud to serve each other. Today we don't wash each other's feet—but what are some of the other ways we can serve each other?

I have another picture here of hands holding bread. That reminds us of another way to follow Jesus. What does he want us to do with the bread? (*Asks children about world hunger, etc.*) It's hard to think of being hungry when we eat well every day, isn't it?

Are some people hungry for things other than food? How about love, acceptance, attention?

I know a little girl named Katie who would stop and talk to a neighbor who didn't have any family to visit her. Katie would tell her about school and tell the woman her flowers looked nice. Katie was feeding the hungry. What was the woman hungry for? *(Waits for response)*

A good sheep, a good follower, actually, looks for ways to serve others. We need to be on the lookout for our chance to help.

All of this helping seems like a lot of work, doesn't it? Yes, it is! But the secret Jesus knows is that this type of hard work makes us happy.

Did you notice that your sheep are smiling? Right! All good followers of Jesus discover real happiness when they feed the hungry, clothe the naked, visit the sick and imprisoned. Grumbling, grouchy sheep are not true followers, so let's put our happy sheep in our hearts and up on the wall/easel where they can follow the leader.

After you have put your sheep up, you may return to your seats.

COMMUNAL PRAYER

PRAYER LEADER   The response to our petitions which today are composed by the children is "I will follow you, Lord."

SONG LEADER   "Come and Go With Me" *(Hi God II)*